Kissinger
on
Kissinger

Kissinger
on
Kissinger

Reflections on Diplomacy,
Grand Strategy, and Leadership

Winston Lord

ALL
POINTS
BOOKS

www.allpointsbooks.com

Library of Congress Cataloging-in-Publication Data

Names: Lord, Winston, compiler.
Title: Kissinger on Kissinger : reflections on diplomacy, grand strategy, and leadership / [compiled by] Winston Lord ; introduction by Henry Kissinger.
Description: New York, NY : All Points Books, 2018. | Includes index.
Identifiers: LCCN 2018057769| ISBN 9781250219442 (hardcover) | ISBN 9781250219459 (ebook)
Subjects: LCSH: Kissinger, Henry, 1923—Interviews. | Statesmen—United States—Interviews. | United States—Foreign relations—1969-1974. | Diplomacy. | Leadership. | International relations.
Classification: LCC E840.8.K58 L57 2018 | DDC 327.730092 [B]—dc23
LC record available at https://lccn.loc.gov/2018057769

Our books may be purchased in bulk for promotional, educational, or business use. Please contact your local bookseller or the Macmillan Corporate and Premium Sales Department at 1-800-221-7945, extension 5442, or by email at MacmillanSpecialMarkets@macmillan.com.

First Edition: May 2019

10 9 8 7 6 5 4 3 2 1

For Bette

Contents

Introduction

by

HENRY A. KISSINGER

*"Everything depends, therefore,
on some conception of the future."*

Two years after I wrote that this principle should shape America's foreign policy, President Nixon asked me to serve as his national security advisor. Given our histories with each other, the opportunity was not one I had expected. But the imperative of a conceptual design for the conduct of foreign policy was a conviction Nixon and I shared.

In 1969, the Nixon Administration inherited a perilous landscape at home and abroad. We strove to tackle these challenges with strategic vision. While I have written extensively about our journey, this presentation of it is informal and colloquial; it is my sole oral history. I did not expect its evolution. Winston Lord and K.T. McFarland persuaded me to participate in an hour-long interview to cap a series of videos about Nixon's foreign policy. Their preparation and determination prompted five more sessions.

Like all oral histories, this is a brief for my case. I did not go out of my way to be self-critical. My interlocutors have been my colleagues and friends for many decades. But they probed the contentious. Their objective was to distill my views on the key foreign policy issues of the years 1969 to 1974, and to do so in a fashion that interested the generations that succeeded us, for whom this period may seem like ancient history.

This is, however, more than a recollection of milestones. It offers insights into my relationship with President Nixon, and the arts of leadership, negotiation, and the making of foreign policy.

Due to the provenance of these interviews, they cover only my years of service under President Nixon, who, after a landslide reelection, was poised for a truly promising second term, particularly in foreign policy. We had opened China. We had made progress with the Soviet Union. We had made inroads in the Middle East. But Watergate, Nixon's resignation, the erosion of executive authority, and the resurgence of congressional custody placed enormous demands on the Ford Administration's effort to sustain America's credibility. Under President Gerald Ford, we managed to retain the thrust of our relations with Beijing and Moscow, progress in the Middle East, reshape our policy in southern Africa, and explore the coming challenges on the global agenda.

Though much has been transmuted since that era, many of its guiding tenets remain relevant. Some should be considered anew. America's foreign policy should proceed from strategic blueprints rather than reactions to discrete events. Statesmen must make courageous decisions with imperfect, often ambiguous information. In negotiations, America's point of departure should be a clear exposition of its needs and an understanding of its interlocutor's history, culture, and goals.

Above all, what has not changed is the indispensability of American leadership. Its exercise compels us to integrate our interests and values—as I wrote in my first book, *A World Restored,* more than half a century ago, to "attempt to reconcile what is considered just with what is considered possible."

Foreword

This book is the written version of Henry Kissinger's one and only oral history, and it came about more or less by accident.

Several years ago, starting in 2014, K.T. McFarland and I agreed to steer a series of foreign policy panels for the Nixon Legacy Forums, a joint enterprise sponsored by the Richard Nixon Foundation and the National Archives and Records Administration. They were the brainchild of Nixon Administration alumnus Geoff Shepard, who had organized some three-dozen panel discussions with former White House officials to reflect on the thinking and processes behind the various domestic and foreign policy initiatives of the Nixon Administration—collective oral histories, if you will.

Many of the panelists had already done individual oral histories but had not appeared together in a group format. The idea was that the whole would be greater than the sum of the parts; that the panelists would build off each other's recollections to create a more complete picture. The sessions were recorded, shown on C-SPAN's American History TV channel, and the videotapes made available through the Nixon Foundation.*

K.T. and I ran four foreign policy panels from 2014 to 2015: "The Revitalization of the National Security Council"; "The Opening to China"; "Soviet Détente and the SALT Negotiations"; and "Vietnam and the Paris Peace Accords." These, together with an earlier panel on the Middle East, covered the major foreign policy initiatives of the Nixon-Kissinger collaboration.

I wrote the outlines for each discussion, which were circulated to the panelists in advance to refresh their recollections. K.T. led the discussions, drawing staff members out to describe their own experiences and contributions. The original plan was to cap off this series with a one-hour video interview with Dr. Kissinger, for his reflections on these key initiatives.

K.T. and I sat down with Dr. Kissinger in his office in December 2015 for the session. His memory was phenomenal, especially since he is in his nineties, and we were asking him to recall events that occurred half a lifetime before. As the hour drew to a close, we realized we had barely scratched the surface. So we persuaded Dr. Kissinger to do a second interview . . . and a third . . . and so on. He recounted strategic objectives and major milestones, punctuated throughout with personal anecdotes. The interviews became more of a conversation among old friends and colleagues, with the stories Dr. Kissinger told seeming as fresh as if they had happened the day before.

---

* https://www.c-span.org/organization/?66230/Nixon-Richard-Foun dation
https://www.nixonfoundation.org/nixon-legacy-forums/

Early in our exchanges, Dr. Kissinger confided that he had never done an oral history, which surprised us since he had given hundreds of interviews over the decades, and he is clearly one of the most outstanding national security figures of the postwar era. So we teased out our series of exchanges to expand beyond Kissinger's time in government to include his reflections on diplomacy, on grand strategy, and, ultimately, on leadership. In all, we conducted six video interviews with Dr. Kissinger over the course of a year, finishing in December 2016.

We both realized the historic significance of our project—an extensive multipart interview with Kissinger, in his own words, spontaneously from memory and from his own perspective. But these interviews were also important to us personally. I had been constantly at Kissinger's side throughout the period, first at the National Security Council and then at the State Department. K.T. had been the junior-most member of the National Security Council staff, working first as a part-time night shift secretary during her college years and then as his research assistant. Our friendship with Dr. Kissinger has now spanned almost half a century.

The lessons we learned while working for Dr. Kissinger shaped our own thinking over the decades as we both went on to hold national security positions in and out of government. I became president of the Council on Foreign Relations, ambassador to China, and assistant secretary of state. K.T. went on to hold senior positions on the Senate Armed Services Committee, at the Pentagon, as a television news analyst and columnist, and most recently as deputy national security advisor. We, like so many others, have had the benefit of decades of his wisdom.

Our conversations with Dr. Kissinger demonstrated why, forty years after leaving government, he remains widely influential as a best-selling author, pundit, and mentor. During this period, he has met nearly every prominent American and international leader, and they continue to seek his counsel. It is a remarkable performance of savvy, stamina, and sway.

This book represents a transcript of those six video interviews described above. Most of the questions are asked by K.T., and almost every comment is made by me.

K.T. has provided her perspective on what she has learned from Kissinger. I include it below.

* * *

Prior to joining the Trump Administration as deputy national security advisor, I consulted with nearly two-dozen former National Security Council officials for their advice on policies and process. Even though I did it with a view toward the new era, comparisons of the different administrations' approaches to foreign policy–making was natural. The Nixon-Kissinger experience stood out.

Most new administrations come into office and immediately conduct a review of existing national security policies, with a view toward putting their own stamp on policy. Sometimes they have a wholesale change of direction, sometimes they just tinker around the edges of existing policies. But most have approached foreign policy as a series of self-contained, one-to-one relationships, delinked from our bilateral relationships with other countries.

Nixon and Kissinger saw foreign policy as Grand Strategy, where the bilateral relationships are interconnected and interrelated. It was as if they were playing three-dimensional chess, where one move on the global chessboard would have second- and third-order effects on the other countries. I have known Kissinger for decades, but during these conversations I was struck by the sheer brilliance of his mind at work, how he would be discussing one decision made in the late 1960s and then explain how they were taking into account the impact it would have on another country, perhaps years later, and half a world away. By peering into the future in this way, Nixon and Kissinger were able to see opportunities and dangers others might have missed, and were able to use them to America's advantage.

Many leaders see foreign policy only in terms of what they want, giving short shrift to the needs of the other side. Nixon and Kissinger tried to see things from the other country's viewpoint, taking their prejudices, fears, and objectives into account. They recognized that no matter how skilled a negotiator might be, no agreement can stand the test of time unless both sides are invested in its success.

Nixon and Kissinger never lost sight of their Grand Strategy, and saw their day-to-day decisions as fitting within that framework. They were able to stay on course and not get sidetracked when dealing with the routine issues and crises that inevitably arose to crowd out strategic goals. They avoided the trap that many administrations fall into, where the immediate obscures the important. That's why the Nixon-Kissinger foreign policy remains the standard by which all subsequent administrations have been measured.

* * *

I have written brief introductions to each chapter that frame the context and foreshadow key points. The transcript of the video record has been edited for repetition, accuracy, and flow, while retaining the original substance and ambience. As such, it reads like a thoughtful but impromptu conversation, not a polished written treatise. I believe it will not only contribute to the historic record but also provide insights to future generations. Plus, it's a great read.

At the same time, I acknowledge this book's limitations. It is neither a comprehensive nor critical look at Kissinger's and Nixon's years in office. Springing from the Nixon Legacy Forums, it does not cover Kissinger's service during the Ford Administration, which included such major diplomatic forays as the Syrian and second Egyptian shuttle agreements with Israel, and Southern African diplomacy backing majority rule in the continent and paving the way for the independence of Rhodesia and Namibia.

Like all oral histories, this work tells the story from only one perspective. Kissinger himself has written several in-depth histories of the period. Nixon was a prolific writer in his post-presidency years. The archives are rich with memoranda, notes of meetings, and recorded conversations, many of them recently declassified. Historians and journalists have written countless pages on the period. There are dozens of lengthy Kissinger and Nixon biographies, some laudatory, some critical.

While there is much fresh material in these pages, the purpose is not to compete with these earlier works. Instead we bring the reader into the room along with us to hear from Kissinger—in his own words and four decades later—the rationale and decisions surrounding some of the era's main challenges. It is also an opportunity to hear one of our nation's senior statesmen reflect on the larger conceptual themes.

We have done all this with an eye to history, and the younger generations. We are now grandparents, and we recognize these events are ancient history to millennials and beyond, just old books gathering dust on the shelf, mere footnotes to their own busy lives.

For me, those times were all-consuming. This project has allowed me the opportunity to do some reflecting of my own.

* * *

"The Agony and the Ecstasy." That sums up my odyssey with Henry. Whatever my periodic pangs, I always shared the sentiment of Albert Camus: "The struggle itself toward the heights is enough to fill a man's heart." I am deeply indebted to Henry for the climb as well as the view.

Space and scope limit me to brushstrokes.

While stretching my perspectives and capacities, he also stretched my patience and my nerves. Taunting me with, "Is this the best you can do?," before actually, with a sly smile, reading my texts. Exuding disdain for mushy advocacy. Calling on Sundays to demand work on a speech just as the Redskins kicked off. Dismissing my forty-page draft of a white paper on Cambodia two days before the president's deadline. Eighty-hour weeks and lost holidays, birthdays, and anniversaries.

And yes, Henry was prone to occasional outbursts against his staff. But, given the gravitas and pressure of events, this was understandable. Moreover, he usually found a way to circle back with a sheepish gesture to salve the sting.

In short, Henry's screech exceeded his rasp.

Beneath Henry's carapace lies a generous temper. He was not only my mentor and tormentor, but a valued friend.

Henry suffered yes men no more than fools: he selected me as his special assistant after reading several of my papers questioning policies the president and he were pursuing. Then Henry shielded me from West Wing wrath on my first solo stint, a comprehensive report on Laos.

He opened the door for me to attend the exclusive summit in the Forbidden City. He invited me to breakfast privately with a half-starved war protester huddling at the gate to 1600 Pennsylvania Avenue. He included me among a handful of guests when he wed his beloved Nancy. He awarded me, on behalf of my staff, the State Department's highest honor.

Henry extended my horizons—and the sights were sublime. A handshake after a breakthrough toward Vietnam peace in a lush Paris park when colors were changing. From a brutal session via a boozy banquet at a dacha to a nuclear deal in the Kremlin. A seminal speech on majority rule that prompted a tearful embrace from an African president. Shuttling endlessly between Middle East enemies in the world's most explosive region. Skirting at dawn the planet's second-tallest mountain on a clandestine journey toward the earth-quaking China opening.

Along with such scenes, let me sketch Henry's nature.

In his suite at the Waldorf Astoria Hotel, coolly penning a speech amidst the chaos unleashed by the Yom Kippur War. Aboard Air Force Two, above Atlantic clouds, playing Kissinger vs. Kissinger in chess, while he ponders moves for his imminent secret talks with the North Vietnamese. In his corner West Wing office, far from palatial, beaming at the coded assent from the Middle Kingdom to open its Vermilion Gates. On a thunderous helicopter flight to Camp David, bemoaning the gloomy prospect of a lost Moscow summit.

Whiffing ping-pong balls beneath golden rooftops arching to the heavens. Pointing to a chandelier and querying the Soviet foreign minister, with comradely mischief, if that was where he concealed the camera. Checking the overnight scores *of the German football league before turning to the president's daily brief. Touring Disneyland, as he courageously shoulders my not-yet-potty-trained son.*

Almost all eyes in the East Room crowd were glistening except for those of the refugee from the Holocaust holding the Bible, who was forbidden by her son to cry as he became the first Jewish secretary of state.

Thanks to Henry, I feel as Sergeant Kissinger did when he wrote to his parents from postwar Germany: "We thought we had moved worlds and given our youth to something greater than ourselves."

* * *

It is an honor to have collaborated on this enterprise with a towering figure in American diplomacy.

Henry is not without flaws. Who is? In the lyrics of Leonard Cohen's "Anthem," "Forget your perfect offering. There is a crack in everything. That's how the light gets in." I believe history will "ring the bells" of his legacy.

The events—and their protagonist—in these pages summon a seminal passage in my life and a unique period in the journey of our nation.

Nixon-Mao meeting, February 1972. Pictured from left to right: Zhou Enlai, Nancy Tang, Mao Zedong, Richard Nixon, Henry Kissinger, Winston Lord, Wang Hairong.

This is the official Chinese government photo of the February 21, 1972, Nixon-Mao summit, one of the world's most momentous events in the past half century. Yet very few people have ever seen it. Nixon asked the Chinese to hide Lord's attendance in order to spare further humiliation for Secretary of State Rogers, whom he had excluded. Thus Lord was erased from this picture and the meeting's communique. During a subsequent Kissinger visit to Beijing, Zhou presented Lord with this picture attesting to his secret presence at the summit.

Kissinger
on
Kissinger

ONE

Statesmanship

Statesmanship requires both the vision to establish long-range goals and the courage to make the often harrowing decisions to move toward them.

On tactics, the choices reaching a president are close calls—otherwise they would be resolved at lower levels. On strategy, as Kissinger has written, there is the much more exacting challenge of dealing with fateful conjecture. When the scope for action is greatest, the knowledge of the terrain is limited or ambiguous. The more is known, the less the room for maneuver. And the more the assessment differs from orthodoxy, the more severe the isolation.

President Nixon reached toward a hostile power without assurance of its response or that of the American public. He risked a dramatic and fruitful summit by ordering major military operations. He vaulted over a rival's military posture to plant the American diplomatic flag in a volatile area.

Throughout, a core principle of the president was that, since you pay the same price for half measures, you should adopt bold moves.

* * *

Dr. Kissinger, you have had great breadth and depth of experience on the world stage. Essentially, you've known every major leader, statesman, and diplomat for decades, in the United States as well as abroad. You've seen the good, the bad, the successful, and the unsuccessful. As you reflect back, what are the qualities of leadership that you think have been the most important?

The first thing one has to ask is, What is a leader supposed to do? Any leader has a series of practical problems that obtrude and that circumstances generate, and that I would call the tactical level. Beyond that, he has the task of taking his society from where it is to where it has never been. That's the challenge of leadership, to build arising circumstances into a vision of the future.

With respect to the first task, it depends partly on the domestic structure of the society and partly on a certain tactical skill.

With respect to the leadership part, the qualities most needed are character and courage. Character because the decisions that are really tough are 51–49. The obvious decisions get made in the course of bureaucratic consideration. But when you have a very close call, it means that you have decided to go on one road rather than another. So you need moral strength to make a decision on which, by definition, you can almost not have a majority because you're dealing with unfamiliar terrain. And you need courage to walk alone part of the way.

Now, of course you will say, "How about intelligence?" I would say you need a minimum of intelligence to understand the issues. You can always hire intelligent people, but you cannot hire character.

When you talk about character and having to make the tough decisions, are those decisions made by the great leader by himself, or in consultation with, or sometimes against the grain, of his advisors?

That really depends on personality to a considerable extent. From my study of history, most of the key decisions had a personal component that you can say were made by the leader himself. But it's very possible that a leader gains the moral sustenance from a group of friends and advisors whom he really trusts. To some extent, the bureaucratic process can help him, but only to the point of 49 percent, not to the point of 51 percent.

What happens when a decision goes wrong?

Well, if a decision goes really wrong, he has to analyze, first of all, why it went wrong. Because the temptation is to fix what you're doing, to think that a decision goes wrong because you don't achieve what you wanted fast enough. So you try to redouble the effort to speed up the process. Or you discover some specific weakness in the process. But leaders ought to have their mind open to a more fundamental reassessment. That's the first thing you should try to do.

The most courageous and difficult thing is to admit to yourself that you made a wrong judgment here, and then develop the strength and the support to reverse it. But we were never quite in that position. We had things that did not work, but we did not have a course about which we said, "This direction is wrong."

There was tactical adjustment occasionally.

Could you talk a little bit about the role of conjecture, the fact that a leader has to act without being certain what's coming down the road? The longer you wait, the surer you are what's coming, but the less flexibility you have at that point.

Much of the web of decisions is based on conjecture. You have to make an assessment that you cannot prove correct when you make it. You will know it only in retrospect. And the more different your assessment is from conventional wisdom, the more isolated you will be. But as a general proposition, by the time you know all the facts, it is too late to affect them. So the art is to make your judgment at a moment when you have enough facts to be able to interpret what will turn out the correct way, not so soon that you overthrow everything, and not so late that you are stagnating.

You and President Nixon together took a lot of the status quo thinking, the orthodoxy—whether it was the relationship with China, with Russia, with the Middle East—and you rethought them. You used that opportunity to recast, reframe American foreign policy. Talk to us about that process. Did you know you were doing that? Or did you just take advantage of things as they came along? Or did you have some great vision of, "This is where we want to be in twenty years?"

If you look at the process, we had a very active interdepartmental process in which we asked a lot of these sorts of questions. But the interdepartmental process is really geared inherently to the issues that have to be dealt with in a short time frame. That's inherent in the nature of a bureaucracy that daily gets thousands of cables and must frame answers to them.

What distinguished the Nixon-Kissinger relationship was that, for one thing, Nixon did not enjoy bureaucratic discussions. At the level of tactical decisions, he was interested, but not deeply involved. And Nixon didn't like bureaucratic fights, so he focused on discussions of long-range purpose. I was an academic who had written books on the same subjects from an historical point of view, namely not what did people actually do every week, but how did the great leaders analyze the situation?

So, it turned out to be a fortuitous combination. And Nixon and I spent hours together asking, What are we trying to do? What are we trying to achieve? What are we trying to prevent? I had never met Nixon until he was already elected, but we both had had, say, on China, the same idea. He had written an article. I had written papers for Rockefeller in the same sense. So we were agreed from the beginning that we should open to China. We analyzed it in a way that is unique or special in the American process.

In the summer of '69, we became aware that the Chinese had reason to fear a Soviet attack. And how we became aware of it was peculiar to the Nixon Administration. We were studying reports of Soviet-Chinese clashes that came to our attention in many ways, but also the Soviet ambassador kept reporting them to us. From this we drew the conclusion, since the Soviets did not normally inform us about their border problems, that they must be planning something for which they sought to establish a pretext. And we studied the problem, and we studied where the attacks came from and so forth.

The major point is we said to each other, "We may have a decision to make. The Soviet Union may attack China this summer. We have no relations with China. They are permanently hostile. They're attacking us diplomatically and everywhere, but what's our interest in this conflict?" And we decided, and of course that means Nixon decided, that it was against the American national interest to have China defeated, and that it was against the national interest to encourage Russia, indeed that it was in the national interest to discourage Russia.

So we had to find some means of expressing this thought. And we got [Elliot] Richardson, the deputy secretary of state, and [CIA Director] Richard Helms to make speeches. For some reason, this got into a Cabinet meeting rather than an NSC meeting, meaning most people couldn't understand why we were even discussing it. But we had those two speeches that said that if a war starts, it will be a grave matter. That means we'll be involved, at least politically. That was a huge decision that Nixon made. I don't know anybody else who would have made it.

All the top Russian experts at the time warned you and Nixon that if we opened up with China, we'd hurt our relations with Moscow. It turned out to be just the opposite.

Exactly. Now the interesting thing is within the bureaucracy, they just thought it was a stupid move. Some really senior guys who had Russian experience, [Charles E.] Bohlen and [Llewellyn] "Tommy" Thompson, requested a meeting with Nixon. It proved that they were very astute, because they said, "We've been watching your various moves, and we've noted some of the offers you made on lifting trade." Those were nothing offers; they were to permit tourists to buy $50 worth of Chinese goods in Hong Kong. But they noticed it, and they said, "We want to warn you that the Soviet Union will not take this kind of foreign policy, and that you may be starting a war with the Soviet Union." This never got into our system; we didn't work it through the system.

We arranged an appointment for Nixon with these people, and they spent a long time with him. But we decided to proceed even in the face of this warning.

And also it turns out that the China opening improved our relations with Moscow immediately.

So it had the opposite reaction than the one they warned of.

Not then, but later in '71 and '72.

Right. The speeches I mentioned occurred in the summer of '69.

Then between '69 and '71, there was a public hiatus, but a very active diplomacy in which we were first exploring communication channels, and then we used the channels. After I came back from China in July '71, before Nixon made his speech announcing the opening, we informed the Soviet ambassador, in an attempt to forestall a Soviet reaction along the lines that the Soviet experts had indicated, as described earlier. We said in effect, "We are willing to have the same kind of general discussions with the Soviet Union, but we warn you that if you do anything serious, anything confrontational, it will not deflect us and would redouble our initiative." The reply was the exact opposite of what we had been told. The reply was that Soviet Ambassador [Anatoly]

Dobrynin came out to San Clemente to propose a Brezhnev-Nixon summit.

We pursued the Moscow and the Beijing summits simultaneously. Our basic strategy was to be closer to both the Soviet Union and China than they were to each other. The Soviets had misread our earlier attempts to start to have a Soviet summit because they didn't know about the Chinese summit.

And we offered it to the Soviets ahead of the Chinese.

We offered it to them, and they could have actually had it first. And they kept playing us along and kept making conditions. And right up to July 1971 when I was going off to China, the Soviets could have had it first. But they insisted on preconditions, especially with respect to Germany.

As we were flying to China on the secret trip, [Deputy National Security Advisor] *Al Haig called me in Thailand, and with doublespeak, which fooled no one, said that the Soviets have once again turned down a summit.*

So we kept the Soviet summit open, and we would probably have done the Soviet one first, because it would have increased the pressure on China a little more. But then when Russia played their game, we accelerated the China summit. So, by the time Dobrynin came to call on me, being with Nixon in San Clemente, that was about the middle of August, he offered a summit, a need for meetings, a need for a trip by me. And so, in fact, the opening to China facilitated the opening to Moscow and vice versa.

In fact, the Berlin negotiations and the arms control negotiations speeded up right then as well.

One of our assets was that there were a lot of negotiations in abeyance with the Russians. One was the arms control negotiation. The other was the Berlin settlement. The arms control negotiations were of a complexity that was described by [Viscount] Palmerston, then [in the mid-nineteenth century] British prime minister, about a European issue called the Schleswig-Holstein Question. He said only three people had ever understood it. One was dead. The second one's in a lunatic asylum. And he was the third, but he had forgotten it.

Then the same thing happened on Berlin. One of our great assets was that Russia had made an agreement with the Federal Republic of Germany, which sort of recognized East Germany, but it could not be ratified in Germany unless there was a Berlin agreement that guaranteed access to Berlin. And that was a Four-Power matter. On the German side, the advisor to [Willy] Brandt was Egon Bahr, who handled their Russian account from the chancellor's office.

Bahr and I met and set up a system whereby he and the White House would sort of nudge forward a few steps, and then we put the process back into the larger forum. So that started a complex negotiation. There was a three-party negotiation involving the German chancellor, Nixon, and [Leonid] Brezhnev, followed by a Four-Power group involving the four occupying countries and Russia.

The fact that we had a veto on the Berlin negotiation gave us a hold on something that the Soviets needed. And so when Nixon stepped up the military operations in response to the Vietnamese offensive two weeks prior to the Moscow summit in May 1972, the Soviets had to think twice about doing something that would put this complex edifice in jeopardy.

So there were two restraints on the Soviet Union: one was the ongoing Berlin negotiation; and the other was that we had the summit with China. Nixon was able to blockade

Vietnam and resume bombing two weeks before a summit in Moscow. And by the end of the summer, we got settlements from the Soviets: the SALT [Strategic Arms Limitation Talks] agreement at the summit and the Berlin agreement. Soon after we received from the Vietnamese an offer which was the breakthrough in the Vietnam negotiations.

Getting back to the theme of statesmanship, what you've just described seems to me to evoke two other elements. One is strategy, how the pieces fit together in context. Not just tactical, but how what you do in one area affects another and leads to a larger purpose. And, secondly, the factor of courage. Because when Nixon had the summit set up with the Russians, most of his advisors said, "If you bomb Hanoi and mine Haiphong, you're going to lose the summit and all of these arms control and Berlin agreements." And he was willing to, in effect, say, "I'm not going to go to Moscow with our troops and the South Vietnamese getting hit by Soviet arms and not doing something about it." So, it seems to me what you've just described sort of fleshes out some of these statesmanlike qualities.

Yes. But the important thing is really in understanding that Nixon and I were not just sitting in an office and doing all these things. There was a live bureaucratic process going on. We had endless meetings which went through all the contingencies. We thought we knew where we were going. And if we were stopped by the bureaucracy, then we followed Nixon's judgment. We did not let the bureaucracy veto us. That's the important lesson.

Yes, because the conventional wisdom is that the bureaucracy was totally cut out.

You shouldn't get out of this that all the president needs to do is sit in the office and think big thoughts. Those conclusions were the result of extensive discussions and careful analysis. The difference was that if Nixon was stymied for bureaucratic reasons, he would make a leap over it. And his operating principle was, you pay the same price for doing something halfway as for doing it completely. So if you do something, you might as well do it completely. You don't really have a choice to do it halfway.

TWO

Setting the Scene

Every incoming national security advisor deals with two prime factors—the environment that his administration inherits and the president he will serve. While Kissinger was dealt a bleak hand at home and abroad, he was given a strong hand in the Oval Office.

Few periods in modern American history were as tumultuous as the late 1960s.

At home, the country was torn by anguish and anger, division and despair over a bitter war, riots, and three assassinations. Abroad, American credibility was sapped by a consuming conflict and an expansionist Soviet Union. When Harvard professor Kissinger was tapped by Nixon as his national security advisor, he was already one of the country's leading historians and national security experts. President-Elect Nixon had focused on foreign policy, both as a congressman and senator, and most especially as vice president. Nixon complemented Kissinger's background and strengths, held similar strategic instincts, made courageous decisions, and backed his tactical moves.

The two settled on a division of labor and an NSC system geared to the president's operating style. They embarked on a demanding, ambitious foreign policy agenda.

* * *

Dr. Kissinger, when President Nixon took the Oath of Office on January 20, 1969, what was the landscape at home and abroad? These were tumultuous times, not only in the United States, but overseas. How did you see the world?

In the United States, there had been three assassinations. In the previous year, there had been riots in the aftermath of some of these events. There had been demonstrations at the Democratic Convention, of a nature that Chicago was shut down. Abroad, the Soviet Union had just occupied Czechoslovakia. Any negotiations between the Soviet Union and the United States had broken down. The Vietnam War was in its fifth year. So there was stalemate and chaos, and without being partisan, it's really hard to think of anything constructive that was going on. Of course, there was no contact with China at all. It was a very chaotic situation.

I'd never met Nixon when he appointed me in December 1968. We had once shaken hands for three minutes in Clare Boothe Luce's apartment at a big Christmas party, as he was coming in and I was going out, but that was my only contact with him. I had been the principal foreign policy advisor of his main rival, Nelson Rockefeller, and had been for about twelve years.

So, it's astonishing that Nixon had the courage to appoint somebody with whom he had never worked, and who had been in the opposite camp, to what he certainly knew would be the key job, since he was determined to run foreign policy.

If you consider that I spent fifteen years of my life trying to keep him from becoming president, it remains astonishing that he chose me as his security advisor.

A little like his reaching out to Senator Moynihan on the domestic side.

After he got the nomination in '60, he asked me to join his staff.

In 1960, the first time when he ran against Kennedy?

Yes. I turned him down. Then when he got the nomination in '68, he asked me to join his staff. And I, again, turned him down, because I'd stuck with Rockefeller. And then six months after Nixon gets the nomination, he is elected president, and he appoints somebody he, in fact, had barely met, who turned him down twice before, and really never said a good word about him. And he appoints me as security advisor.

How did Nixon see the world? How did you see the world? What were the opportunities that you saw on the horizon?

Nixon had, of course, vast experience in domestic politics, which I didn't have at all, and vast experience in understanding the currents of domestic politics, not only the minutiae of the moment. Secondly, while Nixon was focusing on objectives, he did so in terms of the practical experiences that he had had, and the observations that he had made, in meeting with leaders.

Nixon's approach to foreign policy was extremely conceptual. It had been the field of activity in which he had been most interested. In it he did not encounter the element of opposition that had attached to him through the various campaigns in which he had been involved. He had traveled widely around the world, so when an issue came up, he could identify it with personalities, many of whom he had met. So any problem, Nixon approached from the point of view of, what is the ultimate solution that we're trying to get here? He was restless with tactical discussions, though of course he took an interest in them. He felt the president's role was to achieve the final objective.

So, from the beginning, he would address the question, what are we trying to do here? He had one maxim that I often cite, which is you pay the same price for doing something halfway as for doing it completely. So you might as well do it completely. It characterizes many of his decisions. At critical points, people say, "Oh, look at these crazy guys. They went on alert in a situation." When Nixon made these moves, they were calculated to bring the other side to a point where it would recognize that things were getting very dangerous, and where it didn't want to slide into a crisis by taking marginal steps.

The raw material for my thinking was more historical and philosophical. That is, I saw the world in terms of analogies to historical situations that I had studied, and of the lessons one can draw from them.

So, in that sense, Nixon and I complemented each other. We agreed on what one should focus on. But the raw material for that consideration was different for each of us.

There's another point to be made. When I came in, I was a man associated with the principal opponent of Nixon in the Republican Party, into a White House of associates of Nixon for many years. So one should think of this as my having had a senior staff position at the very beginning, say, the first three months, as a principal staff person. As it evolved with experience, our relative inputs became more comparable. But the final decision was always the president's.

As you reflect back on the strategic vision that you and Nixon had together, talk to us about how you got there, how you shaped events, how you, first of all, arrived at those goals, and then your day-to-day process to make sure that the decisions you were making got you there.

Nixon and I arrived there by different ways. Nixon was basically a loner, so he read a lot. Secondly, he felt more comfortable when he traveled abroad talking to leaders because they were not involved in the domestic disputes that characterized him. So he developed some very thoughtful insights over the years on the operational aspects of foreign policy. I had, for a variety of reasons, made the problem of peace and stability my intellectual concern. So I had read and studied and written books on that subject, but I was never much involved in the tactical decisions.

So it was a good combination. Nixon took a long time to make up his mind, but he was very bold in tactical decisions. I knew the historical context better than he did, so I could add perspective. With all the stories one reads about Nixon and me, we never had a major policy clash. Can you think of one?

No. There were a couple of tactical ones, like how much you get the Russians to lean on Hanoi before you make any other decisions with them, but that's tactical.

Before I went on a negotiating trip, I wrote Nixon an exhaustive memo of the background, of the options, of what I proposed to do. And he invariably read it and made marginal comments. Once I was launched, I wrote him a report every night. I recall very few instances where he ever second-guessed, no instance where he countermanded what we were doing.

I can give you an important example. After the secret trip to China in July 1971, we settled on a trip for Nixon at the end of February. But we thought it was too dangerous to have Mao and Nixon meet without preparation, because the risk of disagreement might be too great. So I went to China in October, four months before the Nixon visit, to determine whether we could agree on the outline of a communiqué. I submitted a draft in the traditional form, stressing agreements. But Mao, through [Premier] Zhou [Enlai], had a different concept. He proposed listing disagreements because it was more credible, and then emphasizing the agreements we did reach.

We were sitting there without communications. I could have gone home. But I felt absolutely confident that Nixon would agree with me. So we reversed what we had come to do, accepted the Mao scheme, and brought it back to Nixon. And he said, "This is terrific. We needed to do it this way." He never questioned one line of it.

So that was a totally different relationship than now with videoconferences.

So, that really was the core of the Nixon-Kissinger relationship: you had a strategic vision that you shared, he gave you a lot of leeway to figure out how to achieve that strategic vision, and then endorsed you and supported you throughout.

But it has to be understood we did not just invent these things. There was a lot of departmental material, but we did

not let ourselves be held up by essentially bureaucratic ob-
stacles when we decided something had to be done.

Now, in the beginning, we had to spend some time on
organizing the system. Nixon assigned General [Andrew]
Goodpaster, who had been Eisenhower's chief of staff, to help
with that. Nixon had no detailed view on what the exact
structure would be, except that he would make the final decisions on foreign policy. So General Goodpaster and I went
to see Eisenhower, whom I had never met previously. I had
had the Harvard view that this was a pretty inarticulate,
maybe slow-thinking, individual.

He was bedridden at the time from a series of heart problems. But he was extremely lively, and with a very expres-
sive face and very clear ideas. So we had a discussion with
him in some detail in which he, Eisenhower, began by saying, "The one basic principle of an NSC organization has to
be that the State Department must not run any interdepartmental group, because they are unable to do that well, and
because the Pentagon will never take orders from the State
Department."

I was agonistic on that point. I agreed with the idea that
the White House should run it, but I had no plan. Under
[President Lyndon] Johnson, the State Department had run
the interdepartmental machinery, such as it was. So on the
basis, really I would say almost exclusively, of what Eisenhower
had said, Goodpaster produced the outline, and Mort Hal-
perin wrote the memorandum of how this might be organized. It took the existing geographic structure and made
the NSC advisor and staff the chairmen of the meetings.

Prior to this, there had been something called interdepartmental groups that were all headed by the assistant secretary of state responsible for the areas. But the way the State
Department works, it's basically producing operational ca-

bles, not strategic guidance, unless the secretary insists that the Policy Planning Staff plays an operational role.

Also, Henry, as you alluded, State was an advocate for specific positions, just like the Pentagon would be, or the economic agencies would be, whereas the White House could be an honest broker for the president.

So Nixon had seen the Eisenhower National Security Council when he had been his vice president, and Goodpaster had been Eisenhower's chief of staff?

Right. And so the memo on which the NSC system was based was fundamentally inspired by Goodpaster and approved by Nixon. I was an innocent in the bureaucratic battles of those times. I was agnostic as to who should chair what. But then it became a huge issue, and the State Department people made strong objections, which increased Nixon's separation from them. And that all happened in the period between the election and inauguration.

So Nixon, from the very beginning, knew he wanted to dominate American foreign policy.

There was no question about it. He had said it in the campaign. But when you say you want to dominate foreign policy, you don't know exactly what that means in an operational sense. For example, the question of who approves the final cables, or at least what does the president reserve for himself, and what can be communicated to other countries. Now, nine-tenths of the cable traffic cannot possibly be approved by the White House, because it would overload it. But Nixon reserved from the beginning, and I strongly supported him, that there were key cables that had to be cleared in the White House. And that usually produced some tension.

So, to go over the logistics of it, or the organizational structure, how did you and Nixon use the National Security Council as the adjudicating body between State, Defense, Treasury, CIA?

It evolved over a number of months. But, actually, we had a very systematic concept, which was implemented from the beginning. We took over the interdepartmental teams. These were the groups that existed for each topic or each area. As I said, we didn't change the structure of them, but we put the NSC in as chairmen. You said as the "adjudicator," but we did not run foreign policy on the basis of watching a process in which we didn't participate.

So we wanted to make sure of two things. That every department got a hearing, and that every point of view would be represented, even if it did not originate in a department. I bet we had more meetings than any comparable administration on the issues of where are we trying to go.

At the very beginning you had this whole series of national security memoranda asking the departments for data and ideas.

Right. We started that process by sending out questionnaires on all principal topics. So then we had these interagency meetings, and they were then distilled into an NSC meeting. But before any NSC meeting, we, of the NSC staff, prepared study memoranda for the president. There were usually two types of memoranda. There was a very full memorandum that stated all of the options as we understood them and the history, and there was a summary memorandum that said, "This is going to come before you at the NSC meeting, and it's going to come before you in the form of these options."

The meetings were conducted in such a way that no decision was made at the meeting. The meeting usually began with my outlining the options. So every department present had an opportunity to say if they thought we in the NSC had not fully represented them. Nixon listened to this debate. There was a discussion, then Nixon would withdraw to study the options. He usually announced his decision in the form of a decision memorandum a few days later.

If I remember it correctly, the papers that went to Nixon were study memoranda that were rather full, but I would say 90 percent of which he read, plus a summary memorandum of at least five to ten pages. There was a discussion, then the meeting would end, and Nixon would withdraw and take the papers with him.

Nixon as a personality was a very solitary type. He did not like a free-for-all argument around him, in which he had to back one side or another. He liked to hear the argument, but he preferred not to be a participant in it, in the sense that he would have to say, "You're right." He liked to absorb it and think about it and then deliver his decision in writing almost like a Supreme Court justice.

So on the practical day-to-day issues, Nixon did not like to see a lot of people who could not add to his thinking. In terms of many other presidents I have seen, he had a more limited day-to-day schedule, and he'd spend a lot of time in a retreat he created for himself in the Executive Office Building.

He used that time to read the material. So I would see him, well, many times during a day, certainly once every day. But there was no formal briefing where we walked in and said, "Here is what happened during the day." It was sort of a continuous conversation, because the probability was that in three times out of five, he had called me during the night or had said come have dinner. So it was a continuing conversation, which you could say was divided up. I would run the day-to-day machinery, and tell him what happened, and sum it up. He did not want to be bothered with a lot of the technical detail. But once it turned into a policy issue, then he would need to know it, and would want to know it. China, was, of course, a top issue. There he would want to know everything.

It seemed to me this approach of Nixon's applied to when you were going off on negotiations too, that you would send him a strategy memo of what he wanted to achieve, and then he would leave the details of the negotiations up to you.

Well, at first it was never designed that I would do the negotiating. That was not part of the original charter. But as it evolved, Nixon realized or developed the view that I knew the details of the bureaucratic situation, and also knew his thinking.

So what Winston said was exactly right. We would write really long memos before I went off, in which we said, "Here is the issue, and here is how it evolved, and here is what we are aiming at, or what we should be aiming at." Then we usually wrote a separate memo that said, "Here is what I intend to say, and here is how we intend to respond." Nixon would make copious notes on these, and comments, which we would of course incorporate. But once I was on the road, I sent him a daily report, and he never interfered. I cannot think of one occasion.

So when Nixon was going through this decision-making process, what did you share with the Defense Department, the State Department?

That depends. The exploration of the actual alternatives, in effect, was shared with all of the departments, because they were part of the decision-making process. You have to remember that this was a period of frenetic leaking. So our process of developing options, which almost always leaked, was very open and transparent. When Nixon wanted to come to a decision, then he restricted the number of participants.

Let me give one example. In maybe the fourth week of the administration, we had an NSC meeting on Middle East policy on a Saturday. Afterwards, Nixon said to me, "The old man would really enjoy it if we both went out to Walter Reed and briefed him on this, and tell him what the issues are." So we went out, and I summarized for Eisenhower what had happened, and Nixon gave his interpretation. He hadn't made his decision yet. This was a Sunday night.

On Monday morning, the whole NSC meeting was in the *New York Times* (the NSC meeting that we had reported to Eisenhower to show him what was going on). I got a phone call from an aide of Eisenhower's, who said, "The general wants to talk to you." Eisenhower used language which I had not previously associated with him, about what a disgraceful performance this was—everything we had told him was highly secret was in the newspapers.

So I said, "Are you blaming me for this?" This led to another outburst that said, in effect, "Keep your feelings out of this. This is your job for your country." So then I said, "We've been here for six weeks, and we've been trying to get this leaking thing under control, and we don't seem to be able to do it." This led to an almost terminal outbreak of rage. Remember, he was at Walter Reed hospital with a heart condition. I think his last words to me were, "Young man, that's one lesson you might learn. Never tell anybody that you can't do the job that has been entrusted to you."

THREE

Opening to China

President Nixon's most salient foreign policy achievement was the opening to one-fifth of the world's population. For half a century, this has transformed global architecture and built today's most consequential bilateral relationship.

Some now see that breakthrough as inevitable, but this judgment seriously obscures the political realities at the time. Washington and Beijing had fought a brutal war on the Korean Peninsula and, for two decades, were locked in mutual isolation and enmity. China dubbed America its archenemy. America deemed China more radical than the Soviet Union.

To transcend this gulf, the Nixon Administration proceeded on two parallel, reinforcing tracks—judicially signaling American intentions in public and securing direct communications with Beijing in secret.

This meticulous process over two years culminated in Kissinger's secret trip to Beijing in July 1971. There, in forty-eight hours, the two sides agreed on a Nixon visit and explored the major issues on the agenda.

* * *

The Nixon Administration, and you personally, are best known for the opening to China. Nixon foreshadowed this in the year before he was elected, in an article he wrote for Foreign Affairs *magazine saying China should become part of the international community. Did you go into the administration thinking the same thing?*

As it happened, we both went into the administration thinking that was something we wanted to do. Nixon's thinking was mostly on the political importance of having China as part of the international system. In the biographies that have been published, you'll see that over the years, as I was exploring Vietnam peace negotiations, I kept running into the Sino-Soviet dispute. So I had more in mind, how to play off China against Russia, although without knowing how to get it done.

I was thinking of China as a road to balance the Soviet Union. He was thinking that if you build an international system, China had to be in it. It's not a significant difference. It's just what our experiences had been. We both decided very early that we would make an effort to get into a dialogue with China.

Nixon sent you a memo on February 1 to this effect, one week after the inauguration.

Yes. It was a fixed principle, and we both, whether you approached it his way or my way, believed we had to start with talking to China. So this was in both of our minds.

The significance of this is that Nixon had made his career as an anti-communist. Also, the conventional wisdom was

that the Sino-Soviet alliance of the world's two largest com-
munist nations was impregnable. When did you and Nixon
see that there might be a crack in that alliance, and an open-
ing for the U.S.?

We got real momentum behind this thinking, I would guess, around April, May, of the first year, '69. There were a series of clashes between Soviet and Chinese forces on the Chinese-Soviet border, and we asked somebody from the RAND Corporation to give us a briefing on the significance of these clashes. In getting a map of these clashes, it appeared that most of them occurred near Soviet strong points, and far from Chinese points, from which we deduced probably the Soviets were the aggressors.

The Soviets made their own situation more complicated by briefing us on these clashes. We weren't used to the Soviets briefing us about their problems. So then we thought, "Maybe they're trying to create a pretext for an attack on China." It later turned out, we now know from Chinese documents, that the Chinese took it so seriously that they sent most of their ministers into the countryside.

So during the summer of '69, we took a position. Nixon and I debated, assuming there was a conflict, where do we stand? We came to the conclusion, which was sort of a balance-of-power one, that if you don't know what to do, support the weaker against the stronger. At a minimum, we did not want China to be occupied like Czechoslovakia. So we asked a number of senior people in the administration—CIA Director Dick Helms and Deputy Secretary of State Elliot Richardson—to make speeches saying that we would not be indifferent to any attempt to conquer China. At the same time, we were trying to find a place from which we could talk, or find a channel to Beijing.

I think it's also important to remind people the United States had no diplomatic relations with China for the previous twenty years.

And China had virtually no diplomats abroad because they had been recalled during the Cultural Revolution. We went to Charles de Gaulle's funeral in April of '69. At the reception at the Élysée Palace, Nixon said to me, "The Chinese ambassador," who was there as the Chinese representative, "if you find him standing alone for a minute, go up to him and tell him we want to talk."

But it never happened, because the ambassador never stood alone. I kept watching for an opportunity. That not succeeding, we came up with the idea that the only other place where it might happen that way was in Poland, because that had been the designated contact point for dialogue with China, although that had not taken place for many years. So we instructed our ambassador in Poland—by "we" meaning I instructed him, of course with the approval of Nixon—that he should walk up to the Chinese ambassador at the next public function, no matter what it was, and say we wanted a dialogue.

The U.S. ambassador thought, "This is another one of these diabolical NSC initiatives running behind the State Department," and he ignored it. He was an outstanding person, incidentally, Ambassador Walter Stoessel. So I asked him to come back to Washington, to the Oval Office. Nixon repeated the instruction, and Stoessel did it at a fashion show in the Yugoslav embassy. The Chinese ambassador was without any instructions whatever, and he ran away, and our ambassador ran after him and handed him this request.

You knew you wanted a relationship with China, but you had no way of communicating. You tried at a reception in Paris at de Gaulle's funeral. You tried through the American ambassador at a reception in Poland.

Also through Romania as well.

So how did you communicate with the Chinese?

Well, we also tried a French channel. We sent somebody who we knew was close to [French president Charles] de Gaulle and who had been ambassador in Hanoi, and therefore knew the communist side of the Vietnam War. We never got an answer out of this, either. At any rate, in a trip around the world in the summer of '69, Nixon spoke to the Pakistani president in the same sense and said we wanted a dialogue.

Knowing that the Pakistanis were close to the Chinese?

Thinking. We didn't know for sure how close they were, and to that we got an answer in about two months after that. Now, in retrospect, to understand it, which we didn't fully at the time, the Chinese thought this was a time that there might be a Soviet attack on them. At one point, [Alexei] Kosygin, the Soviet prime minister at the time, had been in Hanoi at the funeral of Ho Chi Minh in September, and on the way back, on a route around China, changed his direction and flew to Beijing with a message. The Chinese thought he would bring an ultimatum, and thus they responded by talking to Kosygin only at the airport, and only with Zhou Enlai and not to Mao.

And you were able to monitor this? You knew this was happening?

We knew that the meeting was taking place, and we knew that Kosygin had changed his direction. We did not know what the Chinese thought, because we had no contact with them. We thought that, overall, the situation might explode. But we did not know. We did not see the ultimatum part of it, which also didn't happen.

In any event, China and we agreed on a Pakistani channel. Pakistan then relayed the first message from the Chinese to us, and then that evolved over a period of two years into a good five messages altogether via the Pakistani channel.

And in the public debate, this is often described as a dialogue between Zhou Enlai and me. I managed it in the sense of preparing a draft of the answers. But the Chinese were not dealing with me. They were dealing with Nixon.

The Chinese messages were handwritten, and came by messenger from Beijing to Islamabad, and were then carried to Washington.

The Pakistani ambassador in Washington delivered them to your office.

So each message took about a week to arrive. We answered with typed messages on paper that had no watermark on them.

So you could deny it?

Yes. So it took weeks for each exchange, and each exchange on each side was no more than four or five sentences. So each exchange, in a way, was precious. Each exchange was sort of a maneuver. It started with the Chinese saying they were prepared to talk, but only about Taiwan. We would come back and say, "When we talk, each side should be able to introduce its subject. We are prepared to talk on an agenda to which each side can make its contribution."

So this then slowly moved to the Chinese accepting an open agenda.

This was an accomplishment in itself because, for years and years, they said they wouldn't talk to us in any way unless we resolved the Taiwan question first.

There had been 136 meetings in Geneva and Warsaw that all broke up on this issue: the United States would demand that China proclaim that it would solve the problem only peacefully. The Chinese demanded that we agree to the principles of Taiwan returning to China, and that there would be only one China. Since neither side was prepared to grant the condition of the other, these meetings had taken place totally fruitlessly, and Winston is quite right. So this was very significant.

You knew that at the time, the significance of this Chinese concession to agree on an open agenda?

Yes. In fact, the president and Dr. Kissinger wouldn't approve a trip to China by an emissary until it was clear the agenda would be well beyond Taiwan, which implicitly was suggesting the Chinese might be willing to put the Taiwan issue down a longer road. They had other motives, like balancing the Russians and coming out of their isolation.

Let me recall our own internal organizational problems. The previous initiative through Poland culminated in the Chinese ambassador to Poland presenting himself at the American embassy for a dialogue. Actually, two or three meetings took place, which revealed the difference in the bureaucratic approach. This was in a semi-open process, and for each meeting the bureaucracy prepared a long paper on issues that should be discussed, I forget them . . . ten or fifteen items. For each session, the bureaucracy wanted to brief over twenty congressmen and x number of governments.

So Nixon said, "They're gonna kill this baby before it's born!" And while we were cogitating about this, the Cambodia crisis in spring 1970 occurred, in protest to which the Chinese canceled the scheduled meeting. Then we never put it back into that channel.

At the same time, you were doing your White House back-channel?

No. The first months of negotiation were in Warsaw. When the April '70 meeting was canceled by the Chinese, then we did the White House channel. The first attempts at the opening were as I described them. When they led to a dialogue in Poland, it was done in the normal State Department channel. When that stalled, we went back to the White House channel alone.

So how did you get to the point of your secret trip to China in July of 1971?

That evolved through the White House channel. There is another thing to be considered. Nobody in the bureaucracy was very eager to engage in a China negotiation, because they were terrified of congressional reactions, and they were terrified of media reactions. Not that the media would be hostile, but that they would force them into a lot of explanations. So when the channel stalled in Poland, I don't recall a single occasion that the State Department came back to us and said, "Shouldn't we try to go back to the Chinese?" They seemed to be quite happy that things were dormant for a while.

And as we discussed, some of their Russian experts were worried it might hurt relations with Moscow.

Exactly. That's a very important point. As this channel was evolving, the thoughtful experts in the State Department, especially the Russian experts, realized the implications for Sino-Soviet relations, and two of them—Bohlen and Thompson—called on the president to warn him that if he pursued this policy, and if he succeeded as they thought he might, this would lead to war, because Russia would not accept it.

So did you and Nixon understand that by having a relationship with China, it would not hurt your relationship with the Soviet Union, but in fact might improve it?

We didn't understand that at all at first. We thought [Moscow diplomat George] Kennan, Bohlen, and others might be right.

But there were a number of principles we believed in. One was the one Winston mentioned before. We did not want Russia to be the sole spokesman of the communist world; we wanted to split it. Second, we wanted to engage in an initiative that showed that we had a global view, and not just the regional view of Vietnam. Third, we thought we might, if it worked, balance China against Russia. And we believed that these objectives were so important that Nixon was willing to run the risk of Soviet displeasure. We did not know how the Soviet Union would react.

Nixon did what he always did in these situations. He would take the risk. He said he proceeded against the warning of those ambassadors, because he thought we could not put ourselves in a position where the Soviet Union could control the communist world by the threat of occupying those countries. Therefore in the summer of '69, when there was the threat of a Sino-Soviet war, we did what nobody had expected. We made formal statements that indicated that if there were a war, we might sympathize with the victim of the attack, even though we had no diplomatic relations with it.

And certainly in our backgrounding as well.

And also in our backgrounding.

Not that you would sit it out, but that you would in fact potentially help the Chinese?

This sent a signal both to China where we stood, and also to Russia. So it was very useful. It seemed to me one last advantage of the opening, as it turned out, was that we knew even then that whatever the outcome of the Vietnam War, it was going to be ambiguous and not going to be a World War II–type victory. So for the American people the pain of that outcome could be eased and put in perspective by the dramatic opening to one-quarter of the world's population. It would also help to free up our diplomacy and show the world we weren't crippled by the war.

Right.

Did you have any idea, when you went to China, and then when Nixon went to China, that it would have such a profound impact?

Yes. We knew that this was one of the most dramatic events. But when I left for the secret trip to China, we had no idea what exactly would be awaiting us, because all we had agreed was that each side would present its views.

When you were pursuing the relationship with the Chinese, in the early stages that you just described, what was going on with the U.S.-Soviet relationship?

The Nixon policy was to maintain both relationships and, in fact, we were planning two summits. One with each of them. Actually, initially we would have preferred a Russian summit first, and we began exploring it with Russia, which of course did not know we were planning a Chinese summit. The Soviets thought that they could use Nixon's apparent desire for a Moscow summit to blackmail us into some concessions in their German negotiations, the recognition of the German postwar borders.

We turned that around by linking it to the Berlin negotiations. At any rate, when it became apparent that the Soviets were trying to use the summit to extort more than we were prepared to give, we put all our emphasis on the Chinese summit first.

We even offered to the Russians the summit first, once again as we were traveling toward China, and they turned it down. Then we went into China. But the interesting thing is—

But we were planning it simultaneously.

Right, and as soon as your trip to China was announced, within weeks the Russians agreed to a summit.

Yes. They agreed to a summit.

So we got their attention.

So you turned the tables on them. They thought they would exploit you, and you turned out to exploit them?

Yes. But the important thing is that Nixon went that route even while he thought there might be a Sino-Soviet war, and even though he thought that, at one point, both summits were in the air, and we might have lost them both.

What was it like at the White House at that point? You've got everything riding on a China summit, and a Soviet summit, and they could both collapse. Was it a tense time?

Well, we thought, if you read the Chinese documents carefully, they were definitely moving toward opening to us. At any rate, that was our conviction. But it was a precarious time.

And the Chinese also felt isolated. I think they figured if they opened with us, then Europe and Japan would come on board. They'd get into the United Nations. In addition to balancing the Russians, I think they were trying to use us to get out of isolation.

They certainly had their own objectives. But their dominant fear for the first few years of our relationship was an attack from the Soviet Union, and they wanted us as a counterweight without admitting that this was their objective.

So the relationship was this: the United States had its objectives; the Chinese had their objectives. They coincided. The Sino-Soviet division you were able to recognize early on, and exploit.

If you look at the beginning of the Nixon Administration, and somebody had said that within a limited period of time, we are going to have improved relations with both the Soviet Union and China, and then we're going to have a big array of negotiations with the Soviet Union after we have opened to China, people would have said, "This is an absolute fantasy."

Did the Soviet Union think that there might be an opportunity for the United States and China to improve their relations?

Yes. Well, the interesting thing is when I became convinced that we could not win the Vietnam War the way we were going, I, on my own, as part of international study groups out of government, went to various East European research groups to see what they thought about a negotiated settlement. In those discussions, it emerged that in Czechoslovakia, for example, they were terrified of a Sino-American improved relationship, because they thought this would lead to a crackdown by the Soviet Union in Eastern Europe.

So therefore, when we came into office, that thinking had been embedded in my own approach.

So in your own thinking, you had already begun to see that there was an opportunity that you could open to China?

I theoretically thought that, yes. I had learned that there was some basis for it. But I didn't know enough about Mao, frankly. I had accepted the conventional thinking. When Winston and I were on the way to China, the CIA published a study on China in which they listed all the reasons why China might want to move toward the United States, but pointed out that none of this could happen while Mao was alive.

Also, the Soviets tried to get us to line up with them against the Chinese in the '69 crisis.

It's really important to understand about Nixon that all this time we were navigating between potential catastrophes. I mean, supposing they had exhibited me in China and said the Americans came to surrender, or to give up their claims. Nixon would have been destroyed. He would have fallen into a trap. Whatever his expressions were, he was very calm about maintaining the American position in the face of difficulties.

We never went off in July 1971 being told by Nixon, "Now be very careful." When we went off, we were told, "Get this done." I never had any means of communicating with him while I was in China.

It's very difficult for anyone to understand that in those days we had no relationship with China at all. While you were there, you couldn't communicate with the White House.

We could not reach Nixon. I do not think we could have reached him by even open telephone. They didn't have the technical means.

While we hoped that we could arrange a presidential visit, it was by no means assured before we took off. That's why you needed this first secret trip, to explore the terrain rather than exposing everybody to a potential catastrophe.

If you look at the transcript of our conversation of the first two days, Zhou Enlai and I sound like two college professors discussing the nature of the international system.

So on Saturday evening, we had about twelve hours left. The meeting ended because Zhou had to go to a dinner. I said, "How should we spend the evening?" He said, "First, we will have to say something about the visit."

I said, "What visit?"

He said, "Both visits."

So then we knew we were going to have an invitation to the president. But then Zhou disappeared, and we had to draft.

And the issue was, they wanted to make it look like Nixon was eager to come to China, and we wanted to make it look like China was dying to have Nixon.

Exactly. That was unresolved when we went to bed, and wasn't resolved until two hours before we left.

FOUR

The Nixon-Mao Summit

Never before or since has there been a diplomatic document like the 1972 Shanghai Communiqué that crystallized the president's visit to China. Unique in sentiment and structure, it is still invoked today.

The summit produced both immediate results and lasting reverberations. The essence of the breakthrough was to finesse differences through unilateral statements, postpone the resolution of intractable problems, and, against this candid backdrop, address shared strategic objectives.

The outcome met the classic precondition for a successful negotiation—victory for both sides. China emerged from the diplomatic isolation of the ongoing Cultural Revolution and gained a sense of security against its threatening northern neighbor. The United States engaged this great nation while preserving political and security ties with Taiwan, produced immediate breakthroughs with Moscow, and enlisted help on the Vietnam negotiations.

More broadly, Washington demonstrated diplomatic

acumen amidst domestic and foreign travails and lifted the morale of the weary American people.

* * *

The United States and China had not talked to each other for twenty-five years. How did you prepare President Nixon for the trip?

The security advisor has to understand how the president works. There is no abstract way the security advisor can know that. We had experienced, by that time, that Nixon was prepared to read voluminous reports; that he prepared himself for meetings with anybody, but would especially prepare for something of such historic significance, by reading as much material as we were able to assemble.

The major responsibility for assembling the materials was Winston Lord's. We did a number of think pieces, which were drafted by Winston and reviewed by me, and he collected all the material. And so Nixon had big briefing books in preparation for the visit. In addition, our NSC team and I had paid an October visit to China between the secret visit in July 1971 and Nixon's visit in February 1972, on which we began drafting the communiqué. And the reason for that was that we did not want, and obviously the Chinese also did not want, a situation in which the drafting of the communiqué would be pushed into a three- or four-day period of the summit, and tensions might develop that would be difficult to control.

So in October 1971, Winston Lord and I and the same team that had been on the secret trip, augmented by the advance team of Nixon's that prepared the actual physical accommodations, went to China for a relatively long period, I would think about a week, and we started drafting what came to be the Shanghai Communiqué. We had brought a conventional-type communiqué with us stating a lot of vague agreements and generalities. My recollection is that at first Zhou Enlai seemed to be willing to work on a communiqué of this kind. But he came back the next day and said that Mao thought it was all nonsense.

We actually gave Zhou Enlai a draft, and he went away and came back the next day.

That's right. We gave Zhou Enlai a draft, and that's what I meant when I said he did seem to be willing to discuss that. As we discussed before, he came back the next day and said that Mao totally rejected it because it created the wrong impression, and that the best thing to do would be to draft a communiqué in which each side stated its contrasting views as clearly as they could and then list a few agreements. He thought that this would be, one, an accurate reflection of the situation; and, secondly, it would make the agreements that we did reach stand out.

This visit in October took place, moreover, within a couple of months of Lin Biao's ouster. [Lin Biao had been Mao's designated successor since 1969.] When we arrived at the state guesthouse, we found a number of pamphlets about "America the Imperialist." We collected all the documents, and our staff gave them to one of their protocol people and said, "These papers were left by a previous guest's group." The next day, Zhou Enlai said, "Remember, we sometimes fire empty cannons." Zhou had made it clear that he dissociated himself from those pamphlets.

So had those been left deliberately by the Chinese?

Certainly. It is inconceivable it could have been an accident.

Getting back to the communiqué, the proposal to state disagreements as a way to highlight the key agreements is one of those ideas that when you see it, you will say to yourself, "Why didn't I think of something like that?"

Now, we were in a difficult position, because here we were sitting in Beijing, and we had no day-to-day communications with Washington. They were proposing to change the whole structure of the communiqué. But I had the confidence that, whatever Nixon might say behind the scenes to individuals, he never failed to back up a negotiation that was conducted with his authority. So I was confident that if we came to a conclusion of the best way to proceed, that he would back us. Secondly, I was quite convinced that he would agree that it was a good idea.

Also, by having each side state its views, the communiqué was not only made more credible and also reassured our domestic publics, but it didn't make our respective allies nervous that we had reached some kind of secret view. It had never been done before.

There has never been a diplomatic document that was drafted in this manner or had that structure.

You said earlier that Nixon would have an idea of the strategic goal he wanted, but left it up to you to figure out how to achieve it. What were the goals that Nixon had in the trip to China and in the Shanghai Communiqué?

With respect to long-term goals, Nixon and I were on the same page. Nixon was more conscious of the domestic impact than I would have been. But we had gone through a number of years of bringing before the American public a vision of peace in Vietnam, and he saw the enormous benefit for the American people to understand that they had a presidency that had a vision of peace in the world. And so that was an aspect of it that was uniquely Nixonian. He and I were both clear about the impact it would have on the Soviet Union.

And we had not yet worked out in detail how what was started as a one-time impact could become a permanent feature in service of putting ourselves in a position where we would be closer to both China and the Soviet Union than they were to each other. But we had foreshadowed it in the annual presidential reports that we drafted [published each February] and that Nixon approved and absorbed. That was a unique aspect among the presidents that I've dealt with, this deep absorption into the subject.

In what way was the Shanghai Communiqué a unique document? How was it different from other documents or communiqués of summit meetings?

Here were two declared adversaries that were meeting at the presidential level and producing a fairly lengthy document that went through a whole set of issues, and it would say the American view is . . . the Chinese view is . . . And on a number of issues, those views were quite contrasting. Each side was free to state its own views, but each side permitted the other to comment on its version.

There was one instance where I said to Zhou Enlai, "If you modify this sentence, we will give you a sentence in our part." He said, "I don't want that. If you can convince me to modify this sentence, you don't have to give me a sentence in your section." It was the method in which it was negotiated, and it was very good for both sides. We could state different views on Vietnam, we could state different views on a number of things, but it was ideal for the handling of the Taiwan issue, because it made it possible to affirm One China without a final determination.

For us, the problem was how to recognize One China without at the same time withdrawing recognition from Taiwan, which was still a recognized country and an ally. So we came up with a formula, and we have received a lot of credit for it. But I lifted it from something that Alex Johnson [Ambassador U. Alexis Johnson] had proposed to [Secretary of State John Foster] Dulles in 1954, which I found when I went through the State Department papers.

In 1954, Alex Johnson had proposed to Dulles that America should handle the Taiwan problem by saying both sides of China in the Chinese Civil War recognized that there is only one China, and the United States would not challenge the proposition. I put it forward as our proposal.

So in other words, we didn't accept it, but we just did not challenge it.

So you could each refer to "China," but each have a different China in mind?

Yes, we said both sides in the conflict asserted that there's only one China, and then we added that the United States does not challenge that proposition. This was in our unilateral statement. Their unilateral statement read further, but by attaching themselves also to our unilateral statement, we could take a position on Taiwan which managed to navigate the period ahead of us, affirmed the principle of One China, but did not require us to determine at that point who represented the One China.

That sentence was not agreed to in the previous visits, only during the Nixon visit.

It's fair to say the October visit settled most of the communiqué except for the Taiwan issue.

We left the Taiwan issue open. Although the concept was discussed, we didn't formally introduce it until the summit.

Wouldn't you say, Henry, that the Chinese made major concessions on this issue? For years, they had said, "We have to settle this issue. It's the only agenda item." They moved all the way to the situation where we opened up with them while postponing the issue.

And still having troops in Taiwan.

Still having troops which we said would only be removed if Vietnam calmed down, to give China an incentive to deescalate the Vietnam War.

That's right. We linked Taiwan to the settlement of Vietnam when we linked the withdrawal of our troops from Taiwan to the settlement of Vietnam.

The last point is, in your press conference at the end of the Nixon visit, having alerted Zhou Enlai in advance, you affirmed our treaty commitment to Taiwan—while on Chinese soil. So, of course, we had to move on China in terms of the One China principle, but the distance the Chinese moved was extraordinary.

And did you know that they would have that flexibility going into the summit?

When we arrived in China in October, we knew from our July visit that they were eager to settle. When we went with Nixon in February, we knew that we had the text of the Shanghai Communiqué minus the Taiwan section. But we were quite confident that we would get it concluded. The most difficult part of the Shanghai Communiqué came after we had concluded the discussions, and Nixon and Mao had signed off on it—the drawback was that no one in the State Department had seen it.

And so on our second-to-last night in China, we were in Hangzhou, we thought it was all over with the communiqué finished. And then we showed it to the State Department. And inevitably, somebody who has an interest in the nego-tiations and didn't participate in it thinks they could have done better, because they don't know all the context in which it emerged. So the State Department raised a whole host of what I thought were extraneous issues. For example, we had said in our draft all Chinese on both sides of the Taiwan Straits say there's only one China, and the United States doesn't challenge the proposition. The State Department said, "How do you know all Chinese have that view?" They had numerous nitpicks, and we took this to Nixon while he was dressing for dinner. Nixon said he would stand behind the communiqué as it was drafted and, if he had to, he would absolutely insist on it. But if we could get, I forget, ten to fifteen of the relatively minor changes proposed by the State Department, it would help him greatly.

So after dinner in Hangzhou, I asked for a meeting with Zhou Enlai and told him that the text approved by Nixon and Mao had to be reopened. And there was an explosion, as you can imagine. But finally, he said, "Why don't we attend to it?" And so we went through the document and found—I don't know how many places—where the Chinese were willing to make adjustments that probably improved the document somewhat. But these were not major issues.

So did the Chinese think you were trying to renegotiate the communiqué?

Yes, because we did. But I explained to them that, "If you insist, we will stick with the document. But it will make it that much harder to sell in the United States." And one of the associates of Zhou Enlai, who later became ambassador to Washington, had a fantastic English vocabulary. He was a genius in finding an English word that would meet the requirements of both sides.

There was one issue where we had reaffirmed all our alliances except our alliance with Taiwan. And the State Department was correct to suggest, "Let's not reaffirm any," so Taiwan doesn't stick out. So you deleted all references to alliances and reaffirmed the Taiwan one in the press conference the next day. That's the only significant one, I think.

Yes. I'm not saying the State Department was wrong. Many of their suggestions were useful, though not material.

Yes. That was the only one.

They were the sort of things that would come up toward the end of a negotiation, as you go through the scrubbing process. But at any rate, it was a dramatic event. We didn't get finished with it until four in the morning. And the release of the communiqué was scheduled for around noon.

A key point we got in the Shanghai Communiqué was an anti-hegemony clause directed at Moscow, which is one of the areas we did agree on.

That anti-hegemony clause was one of the most important points from the Chinese perspective. But it was important also from our perspective. That China and the United States agreed that neither of them would seek hegemony meant there would be no Chinese incursions anywhere. And, secondly, that we would oppose the efforts of any other country to achieve hegemony. In day-to-day policy, it was more important than the Taiwan clause, which just enabled us to do business.

So when you left the summit, did you feel that you'd gotten what you had come to China for?

There is, I think, in the archives of the Nixon Library, there has to be a record of the conversation Nixon and I had in his hotel room at the end of this trip, in which we summed it up as having changed the old strategic balance but, above all, as giving new hope for the world.

And let me say something about that conversation. You know, it's very hard to present Nixon in a human way because he was so remote except to the few very close to him. But this conversation is a good example of where he was at the end of a great triumph, not elaborating on what he had done, but asking what does this mean for America and the world.

And I think there was a positive reaction in the United States, thanks to the television coverage.

Yes. But he did not know that impact while we were negotiating.

He didn't know, and flying back on Air Force One, we were worried about what the reaction would be in the U.S.

Did you have any idea what was happening back in the United States?

I had a terrible time on the trip back to Washington, because Pat Buchanan [a conservative staff member] was on Air Force One, and he blamed me for an imminent disaster, which is wrong. It was a deep commitment to Nixon. And, no, we didn't know what we would find. When we got back, it turned out to be a much better reception, even among the conservatives.

What was the impact on our allies, particularly Taiwan?

Taiwan could not be enthusiastic about this. And for Taiwan, the major concern was how to cut their losses and how to survive in this new environment. We attempted to give them every assistance in adjusting to circumstances.

The major impact we were watching was the Soviet Union.

FIVE

Seeking Stability with the Soviet Union

The Cold War between nuclear superpowers compelled the United States to reconcile two moral imperatives: in the words of Kant, "The obligation to defend freedom and the necessity for coexistence with adversaries." We would never give up core principles, but we could not maintain them unless we survived.

For two decades, the United States and the Soviet Union had engaged in a global competition, punctuated by genuine crises. The Nixon Administration, in the first two years, resisted pressures but made scant progress in easing tensions. The Soviet nuclear arsenal was growing, and talks on various fronts were stalled.

The opening to China broke this logjam, spawning rapid progress toward a summit, arms control, and a Berlin agreement. The president's visit to Moscow in May 1972 produced major agreements.

Nixon and Kissinger thus realized their goal of pursuing better relations with each of the two communist giants than they had with each other.

Inevitably, the rivalry with Moscow endured. But the Nixon Administration left a more stable relationship to succeeding ones, which labored in turn for a peaceful victory in the Cold War.

* * *

At the same time you were talking to China, you were also in negotiations with the Soviet Union on arms control and a Moscow summit. How did the opening to China affect relations with the USSR?

We had had a whole series of negotiations with the Soviet Union. Our original plan was to combine those into a summit, and to use that summit with the Soviet Union to create additional incentives in China. But then the Soviet Union tried to, in effect, blackmail us with the prospect of a summit and dragged it out. So we reversed the process and said, "Okay, we'll go to China first," which the Soviets had never contemplated.

We were not sure what the Soviet reaction would be. As Nixon was starting the opening to China, as I said, a group of senior Foreign Service officers had warned that this might lead to a conflict with Russia. So that warning remained in our minds when I took the secret trip to China in July 1971. Therefore, when we informed Russian Ambassador Dobrynin of the presidential speech announcing the secret trip, we attached a very strong warning that we would not be deflected from that course. We did not know whether the Soviet Union would decide to go toward confrontation. But they exceeded our expectations in going toward reconciliation and, within three weeks of the secret visit, they proposed the summit between Nixon and Brezhnev, and changed the whole attitude on every ongoing negotiation.

Had they thought maybe the United States and China would find an opening?

We had seen no official evidence of it. In the biography Niall Ferguson has published, he mentions two conversations I had as a private citizen before I became an official, in which senior communists told me of their anxiety that the Chinese would begin moving toward us, and that this would create a totally new situation. It registered in my mind, but I did not at first think it was as doable as my Soviet interlocutors did.

They moved also on arms control and the Berlin negotiation—the whole pace of U.S.-Soviet negotiations picked up.

Well, one of our great assets with the Soviet Union was that they could not complete their German policy without a Berlin agreement, and they could not get a Four-Power Berlin agreement without our concurrence. So one reason among several why they didn't choose a hard-line response was that they would lose their German policy also.

You had the China summit in February of '72, and you were scheduled to have a summit meeting with the Soviet Union in late May. But in the spring, the Vietnamese war heated up when the North Vietnamese launched an offensive. What was your response to that? How did that fit in with the China and Soviet initiatives?

The North Vietnamese offensive started at the end of March, and culminated at the beginning of April. We had negotiated throughout the Nixon period on Vietnam, but we had warned the North Vietnamese all the way through that if they started an offensive, we would reply massively. While Nixon was in China, we limited our military action against North Vietnam. As soon as the offensive started, Nixon took off all the restraints and ordered a substantial augmentation of our bombing forces.

But the North Vietnamese were gaining ground in Vietnam, because they had thrown in their whole army. In April, I had been in Moscow preparing for the Nixon summit, and I had warned Brezhnev on the specific expectations of Nixon, that if this offensive did not stop, and if they did not withdraw the forces they had recently introduced, we would undertake a serious escalation. We had a negotiation meeting with the Vietnamese, who were very cocky and thought that they had already won. So when I came back from that, Nixon ordered a blockade of Vietnam.

The mining of Haiphong Harbor?

Nixon ordered the mining of all the harbors and an escalation of the bombing campaign. He did that six months before an election, and two weeks before he was supposed to go to Moscow.

Did the Chinese and Russians know that North Vietnam was going to escalate in the spring of '72?

If the Chinese followed Vietnamese patterns, they must have surmised it. I don't think they knew the specific date that they were going to do it, but it was a high probability. We thought the Russians must have known it.

And you had all these experts telling you that the Soviets were going to cancel the summit because of our military response?

The consensus was the Soviets would cancel. In our internal planning in the NSC, we operated from the assumption that the summit would be canceled, and the question was, Should we reschedule another one for maybe a month later, or should we treat it as the end of an effort that year? Yet in the face of these estimates, Nixon proceeded.

A week into the crisis, the Russian trade minister was visiting Washington, and he asked for a meeting with the president. He was not of a level that would normally get to see the president, but we arranged it to see what the Kremlin might be saying. To our surprise, he made it clear that Moscow considered the visit to be taking place, but that was after a week of uncertainty. And it was an enormous Soviet climbdown.

When you responded to the North Vietnamese offensive, did you anticipate maybe you could have hit a Soviet ship in the Haiphong Harbor? Did you anticipate that it might have escalated?

We thought it was a possibility, but not a probability.

I think it's fair to say the president didn't want to go to Moscow not having responded forcefully to Hanoi's offensive, since Moscow was the major arms supplier to Hanoi.

He could not go if Soviet arms had defeated American forces at the end of an extended period of negotiations, which we were conducting with Vietnam. Nixon was absolutely clear that he would not tolerate a North Vietnamese victory.

That took some courage because we had the SALT [Strategic Arms Limitation Talks] agreement lined up and all kinds of other agreements. This was to be a big summit, and he was willing to sacrifice the whole thing.

That's right. He had the SALT agreement, a whole host of agreements.

What was your relationship with Nixon at this point, when Nixon said in effect, "We're going to do it. I'm willing to risk the summit. I'm willing to walk away from that Soviet summit if having it means abandoning Vietnam."

I agreed with him and encouraged him.

You agreed with him even though the entire bureaucracy, all the conventional wisdom said, "No, no, you can't jeopardize this Soviet summit."

I agreed with a drastic response. I did not anticipate that he would order a blockade, but I thought it was a very good move.

What I find in all of the conversations you're having is that Nixon was doing things that may have been politically unpopular in the United States.

Of course.

And yet he was willing to take that risk. He didn't come to you and say, "Henry, I've got to worry about domestic concerns."

No. Nixon asked, "Is it in the national interest? And what are we trying to achieve?" And he had that motto, "You pay the same price for doing something halfway as for doing it completely, so you might as well do it completely." So once Nixon was convinced of the direction of a course, he would usually take the most sweeping solution that was presented to him, or invent one.

What happened at the Moscow summit?

One episode was that Brezhnev "kidnapped" Nixon at the Kremlin and convinced him to go in his car to his dacha! And left the rest of us behind.

At the end of the Kremlin meeting, we were all supposed to follow Brezhnev in an American motorcade. But when we were coming out of the meeting, Brezhnev said to Nixon, "Let's both go together." And so Nixon did what the Secret Service considered unthinkable. He went into a foreign-made car, with no American security, and they took off.

I followed in another car, so I was in the presidential motorcade. But Winston, who had all the briefing books, was left behind. I still don't know to this day how Winston managed to talk himself into a separate car that was permitted to go to the Brezhnev dacha, as far as I can tell, on his own. And he appeared at the dacha.

The first event for Nixon was a boat ride in which Brezhnev drove the boat—a hair-raising experience. But by the time he came back, there was Winston with all the briefing books. The Secret Service was so outraged by what Brezhnev had done that, at the dacha of Brezhnev, it drove its own car under the portico, blocking the door so that the president could not possibly be hijacked again!

Well, the meeting itself was to be sort of businesslike, and then we would go upstairs for dinner. But before dinner started, each of the three Soviet leaders made a long statement castigating Nixon for the escalation in Vietnam and declaring solidarity with the Vietnamese. Nixon occasionally added something, very briefly and very firmly, but did not engage in detailed rebuttals. Then after they had raged on for maybe three hours . . . it seemed endless . . . they felt they had done their Soviet duty.

So they could send the transcript to Hanoi. We then adjourned for dinner upstairs.

Then, the conversation immediately switched to the rest of the issues, of which, at that time, that SALT agreement was the most important. And then Brezhnev proposed that in the spirit of the occasion, [Minister of Foreign Affairs Andrei] Gromyko and I start negotiating immediately. And so we were sent back to Moscow to negotiate, even though it was about two in the morning. We then started negotiating, say, at three thirty. Nixon and Brezhnev had gone to bed.

In short, Brezhnev had announced that in view of the wonderful spirit that existed after three hours of savaging us, we would do exactly the opposite of what they had implied. They had implied they were totally behind the Vietnamese. And so at one magic moment, they said, "Let's eat." And as the eating started, they said, "Well, let's now go to what needs to be done." And then Brezhnev said, "Let Henry Kissinger and Gromyko go off right now." That's when we went off. I know that the sun was coming up when we got to the Kremlin. For some reason, we went back to the Kremlin to negotiate, and we were there for another two hours. And after that, two pretty solid days of negotiations.

So to summarize, the whole summit was quite successful.

It was very successful.

Did you know it was going to be as successful as it was?

We had a big agenda prepared that we had negotiated for a year with the Russians. It was logical to think that they would want to counterbalance what we had done in China by showing that they were a more viable partner. So that was their attitude when the Vietnam offensive started. Once we had made the decision to blockade Vietnam, it looked very dim for the summit. Then when they let the summit go ahead, the presumption was that they wanted to reach major agreements. But if you look at the sequence of the events at the Moscow summit, it was not until after that verbal onslaught that other agreements, there were six or seven agreements, fell into place. And then we had another late-night session on SALT the last night.

The significance of that agreement was that it was the first limitation on offensive weapons that had been negotiated. It led to an intense debate in the United States, but the factual situation was that the Soviets, prior to those negotiations, were producing 250 missiles a year. We were not adding any missiles to our arsenal, because we had concluded that we had sufficient weapons to achieve any rational strategic objective, and that we would not add to our military capacity in any significant way simply by multiplying numbers, and that it was much better to concentrate on improving quality.

So in rough terms, what that agreement did was to freeze the numbers of nuclear offensive weapons at the levels that were reached at that time. It was made as a five-year interim agreement, during which one could negotiate a more complex agreement covering every nuclear weapon and taking into account new technologies. But it was an important first step to reduce international tensions.

In addition, there was an agreement that was designed as a permanent agreement for the limitation of anti-ballistic missile defense. One has to understand that for Nixon, these concessions of limitations were almost entirely theoretical, because there was no possibility of getting the Congress to increase the numbers. The pressures from the Congress were all in the opposite direction.

Also, in addition to outer space, economic, and other deals, there was a separate agreement which reflected a conviction of the Nixon Administration on principles of international conduct. This stated restrictions or restraints that countries should observe in taking advantage of situations like the overthrow of governments and preventing aggression. Now, many of those were theoretical, but they had the advantage that, in a crisis, we could take one of these provisions, if the Soviets violated it, and point out that they were violating an agreement that had been made between the two presidents.

So the summit between Nixon and Brezhnev in '72, occurring at a high point of the Vietnam War, demonstrated one of the main themes of the Nixon Administration: even though we were engaged in a war in Vietnam, and even though the country was torn over the issue of how most effectively to end that war in Vietnam, we saw the possibility of negotiating agreements for world peace and to indicate specific steps toward it. To combine these two actions with

China and the Soviet Union in one relatively brief period of time over months symbolizes the conceptual nature of the foreign policy that Nixon conducted.

Talk about the rationale of détente. Because these negotiations and agreements really put U.S.-Soviet relations on a different track than where they had been before.

The major Soviet decision to start talking with us had come in the previous year. As I said, when we opened to China, we were not sure whether the Soviets would escalate tensions, leave things as they were, or possibly move in the other positive direction, including the summit, SALT, and the Berlin talks.

I think we'd be interested in getting to K.T.'s point about what was the strategy behind détente, whether it's sticks and carrots or linkage, and how did you carry that out? And when it came under criticism, what were the attacks on it? So what was the purpose of détente or the way that we thought we could make progress using it? Is détente well understood by historians?

I don't think that Nixon ever used the word "détente." That's a word that was used by others. And I'm not conscious that I ever used the word until our critics did. The central debate was this: our critics took the position that Russia was an inherently evil state, and they had to be defeated in the Cold War, and that any negotiation with Russia was granting them a moral equivalence and thereby strengthening them in their aggressive maneuvers around the world, and that the culmination of the Cold War had to be some kind of overall diplomatic confrontation or a war.

We took the position that we had defended the free peoples throughout the administration. We had taken a tough stand in the Middle East in the 1970 crisis, we had resisted the installation of a Soviet missile base in Cuba, and we had fought for what we considered a decent outcome in Vietnam on behalf of many countries. So we thought that we owed it to the people of the United States and to the people of the world to show that if a conflict arose, which we had already demonstrated we were prepared to respond to, that if a conflict arose, we had done the maximum to create more peaceful conditions.

And, secondly, if there were elements in the Soviet system that would be willing to coexist on a basis of mutual respect, that we would give them the chance to do that. So we had two tracks to our policy: determined resistance to any Soviet attempt to go beyond the established dividing lines but, at the same time, to ease the confrontation to the extent compatible with our principle to reduce the dangers of nuclear war.

The second or third day in office, I looked at the war plans, because the national security advisor is one of the key advisors to the president in implementing them. And the expected consequences of a nuclear war were threats to civilization that we had not known heretofore. So we refused to accept that we'd simply let these weapons pile up without ever being able to devise a strategy in which you didn't destroy civilization. Those were the impelling motives.

Talk a little bit about the use of pressures and incentives and also the concept of linkage.

The concept of linkage is this. There are always groups, and they're particularly strong in the State Department, whose job it is to negotiate, who hold the view that you can reduce international politics to a set of negotiations, dealing with these negotiations as if they're an end in themselves. There is a danger of drifting into a canon of concessions and of marginal adjustments, where you forget what you're negotiating about to begin with.

So from the beginning, we said that you cannot split up this Cold War into discrete items. And one has to understand that military limitations need to be balanced with commensurate political gains. Linkage in that sense was heavily resisted by the bureaucracy, and we couldn't always stick with it totally. But we managed to maintain the principle so that whenever we negotiated an arms control agreement, we attempted to add to it an agreement on political restraint.

Can I ask one last question? You and Nixon were totally in harmony on most foreign policy issues and strategy, including policy toward Moscow. But wasn't there a little bit of daylight between you on how much to expect out of Moscow in helping end the Vietnam War and how much progress to make on other issues if the Soviets didn't cooperate on that issue?

Well, I'd like to separate two things here. Nixon had the initial view that you could pressure Russia to obtain concessions on Vietnam in one set of proposals. And various attempts at the beginning of the administration to pressure Russia specifically failed. For example, very early in the administration, there was a proposal that we would send Cyrus Vance [later secretary of state] to Moscow with authority to negotiate an arms control agreement with Russia, and simultaneously to negotiate with Hanoi, which would send a representative to Moscow for this purpose.

That effort failed, at a minimum, because Hanoi was more obstinate than the theory implied. And clearly, the North Vietnamese didn't want Moscow to second-guess their negotiating methods. Moscow never replied to this proposal. Dobrynin told me about six months later that they had attempted to put it to Hanoi, and the North Vietnamese had stated that they didn't want any third country to negotiate on their behalf.

So the effort to pressure Russia directly for help in Vietnam did not work. But later on, as we've discussed, the opening to China, which was also a form of pressure on Russia, did have results.

SIX

Searching for Peace in Vietnam

There were two battlefields in the Vietnam War—Indochina and America. The North Vietnamese sought to prolong the fighting in one theater while exhausting public opinion in the other.

Facing this strategy, and inheriting a legacy of mounting troop levels, casualties, and protests, President Nixon weighed all policy options. He decided to relegate ground combat gradually to South Vietnam while we bolstered its capabilities. This winding down of our role would also prop up domestic support. Meanwhile, he authorized Kissinger to negotiate a settlement secretly as soon as possible.

The dilemma was that progress could only be made in talks that were hidden, but because they were hidden, our flexibility and Hanoi's intransigence were veiled from the public as well. Thus, we paid a heavy price in political support, and this in turn fed North Vietnam's obduracy.

* * *

Let's move on to Vietnam. You've set the stage for us in previous sessions where you've talked about the general American political landscape when you came into office in 1969. But let's turn to the Vietnam War, both the situation in the United States and the ongoing peace negotiations. What did you inherit from the Johnson Administration?

And also the military situation on the ground—the troop levels, the casualties, and so on.

In January 1969, we had 500,000 troops in Vietnam, and that number was still increasing on the basis of plans that had been made in the Johnson Administration. So in the first two months of the Nixon Administration, 34,000 more troops were put in on the basis of a schedule that had been established in the Johnson Administration. We had had, at that point, 31,000 casualties in the war. We had a casualty rate of between 500 and 1,000 a week during the Tet Offensive.

The negotiating process had just started, and in fact one of the decisions that Nixon made in the last weeks of the Johnson Administration was to go along with a break of the deadlock on the procedures to conduct the negotiations. He could easily have stopped them and reserved them for himself.

Thus the talks were almost entirely procedural, dealing with the issue of whether the South Vietnamese government would sit in the same negotiation with the guerrilla units that were fighting in the south. There had been no concrete American political proposal put forward in the deadlocked negotiation. The only proposal that the North Vietnamese put forward demanded the unilateral withdrawal of American forces and the overthrow of the South Vietnamese government before any negotiation could start. Those two demands Hanoi never changed until the very end of the negotiations in October 1972.

I mention it only because of the myth that somehow there was some progress available if Nixon had not interfered. It was absolute nonsense. The basic North Vietnamese position was put forward within days of the Johnson bombing halt agreement and never changed. And the key points that concerned us never changed until October 1972.

When you came into office, you knew you had a mandate to end the Vietnam War. Is that fair to say?

In a way. But not on terms that would undermine America's ability to defend its allies and the cause of freedom. Let's remember, the cult of violence in domestic debate really emerged in this form during the Vietnam War. Before then, of course, there were big disagreements between Democrats and Republicans, but the proposition that the government was a bunch of criminal liars who were committing war crimes emerged only at this violent stage. As a result, the mass demonstrations and boycott of public services sought to bring Washington to a standstill. That developed in the Vietnam War.

And also to glorify the enemy as somehow morally superior.

And glorify the enemy. So that whatever move we made, we were accused of acting maliciously to prolong a war that, for some nebulous reason, we preferred to conduct. I had one of my associates once do some research on how long we could get the support of the *New York Times* by carrying out the proposals of the *New York Times* editorial board. At the beginning of the Nixon Administration, it was about six weeks. At the end of the Nixon Administration, it was days.

We'll get to this, but we also paid a price for secret negotia-tions. There were all these propaganda exchanges at the pub-lic talks, so we felt the only way you could make progress was secretly. Not knowing about these talks, critics were saying we weren't negotiating seriously. Thus we paid a price until we finally revealed them in January of '72.

But maybe we should go back to what options we had at the beginning.

Right. So you entered office, and your first goal was to iden-tify and assess the options.

We sent out a list of, I don't know, 130 questions to the key departments, because we generally wanted to get a judgment of where we were. I had been in Vietnam three times before I was given this position, and I knew that there was profound disagreement about the analysis of the situation within the American government. I wanted to bring that to a head and see what the disagreements were, what the factual situation was, and thrash that out. That was the first step.

Then we had a very systematic review of the options as we saw them. And there were essentially three, of which one was a phony option. Option one was withdraw totally, im-mediately. That was ridiculous, because we had been there for four years and were in the midst of major operations. The Joint Chiefs told us it would take us two years to withdraw, even if we were unopposed, under any circumstances. Such an abdication by a Republican president would have been a betrayal of everything he stood for, and it's something that the Democratic predecessors never considered.

When we came in, we found that the existing plan was to withdraw our forces down to a level of 250,000. That's a level we reached within nine months of Nixon entering office. So if you said theoretically: total withdrawal, immediate withdrawal . . .

You'd probably have to overthrow the Saigon government at the same time.

Right. So that was really the North Vietnamese negotiating position. Get immediately out now and overthrow the government.

Of course, you'd be overthrowing the government.

Well, we would by definition.

I cannot think of one significant American political figure, from the left or the right, who proposed that at that time.

So that option was a non-starter.

So then we felt we had two fundamental choices. We had the choice of Vietnamization, which was a gradual withdrawal of U.S. troops while strengthening the Vietnamese armed forces to a point that would exhaust the North Vietnamese, at which point they would then negotiate an outcome.

The alternative, which actually is the alternative that I favored, was to make a sweeping peace proposal, and that was embodied in the Vance mission. Then, if that was rejected, go all out militarily to something like what was done in 1972. We never worked it out completely. We had a study of it under the name of "Duck Hook." How we ever came up with that name, I will never remember. But you read a lot about that in investigative journalists' analyses. This was the follow-on to the rejection of a sweeping peace proposal.

Finally, Nixon decided on the Vietnamization route, and I went along with it, even though my first instinct was that the danger of the Vietnamization route was that the more we withdrew, the more we would be asked to withdraw by the public pressures. And then to synchronize the growth of the Vietnamese capacity to resist with the pace of our negotiations would prove extremely difficult. It was a haunting question that Winston and I knew that [Hanoi negotiator] Le Duc Tho would keep asking, which was, "What makes you think, if you couldn't defeat us with 500,000 troops, you can defeat us by replacing the 500,000 with South Vietnamese troops that are already there?" And we didn't have the answer to that until the '72 offensive, in which we showed them that it could be done with the U.S. in a supporting role.

Actually, we did feel that over time the South Vietnamese ground forces would be strong enough, more or less, on their own. Meanwhile, the American people would see progress being made, and we could thus maintain domestic support for our policy.

You said a few minutes ago that North Vietnam never changed its demand for complete and immediate withdrawal and overthrow of the Thieu government in Saigon. Is that why the negotiations went no place? Because you really negotiated for three years and nothing much happened.

The North Vietnamese were extremely skillful in coming up with slight variations of their proposal, and always exploiting the American domestic situation. There was, for example, one period when the North Vietnamese published a seven-point proposal in the official negotiations and then gave us a secret proposal of nine points. And so we said, "What do you want to negotiate, the seven or the nine points?" "We want to negotiate the nine points." But publicly, they kept saying, "Why don't the Americans answer the seven points?" And we already were in the process of answering the nine points.

A lot of time was spent on these points, and when we got to our key point—are you willing to make a cease-fire, leave the existing government in place, have an election within a very short period of time—they always rejected that.

So we felt we needed to negotiate not only to try and end the war, but also to convince the American people that we were serious about making peace. We were handicapped in this because, as long as the negotiations were secret, we couldn't demonstrate what we had done. But if we made the negotiations open, we would immediately get under pressure from these groups that were demonstrating because we were too tough; they were convinced that the most important objective was to get us out of the war, and they didn't care what the terms were.

You might explain, in May 1971, we made a seven-point proposal that became the essence of the final agreement.

Absolutely. Absolutely.

It shows we could not have reached the final agreement sooner than we ultimately did. It just wasn't possible.

In May of '71, we made the proposal that fundamentally became the final agreement.

Then why did they not accept it at that point?

Because they thought they could defeat us or at least exhaust us.

To understand the Vietnam negotiations, it isn't necessary to go through some of the arcane details. But one has to understand two things: the United States was willing to withdraw, totally, if the North Vietnamese would agree to a political process that gave the South Vietnamese a choice in their own future. The North Vietnamese, from day one, demanded that the United States unilaterally withdraw all its forces at the beginning of the process and that the United States give a terminal date that would not be affected no matter what else happened. And, secondly, that immediately the existing government in South Vietnam should be overthrown and replaced by some kind of coalition government over which the communists would have a veto.

When we, in our negotiations, explored what such a government might look like, we never found a practicing Vietnamese politician outside the government that the Hanoi negotiators considered acceptable. So therefore, they were asking us to stop our military effort and withdraw, overthrow the government on whose behalf we were there, and then the real negotiations would start. That is the only condition we absolutely refused. Every other condition we found ways of accommodating.

Our basic proposal was let's make a military settlement and then have a political negotiation. The political settlement would have recognized the existence of the South Vietnamese government but would have permitted the NLF [National Liberation Front] to participate in the following political process. That's what they rejected until October 1972. Nixon made the May 1971 offer public in January of 1972. Then finally, in October 1972, Le Duc Tho read us a formal proposal which he introduced by saying, "It's what you yourself have proposed to us"; it did, in fact, contain the essence of what we had proposed.

And in fact, at the end of that session, I shook hands with Winston, and I remember saying, "We've done it." That had a great symbolic importance to me, because Winston had wanted to leave at an earlier stage during the 1970 Cambodian incursion, and we had had a discussion: "Will it not be more meaningful in your life if you can say you worked on the peace agreement rather than demonstrated for it?"

So we were deadly serious on our side in doing this, but we were also deadly serious that we would not betray people who, in reliance on our promises, had lost innumerable casualties to defend their freedom. And that is part of the Vietnam War, there is no way of avoiding it. All of the accusations, which started already against Johnson and continued against Nixon, we've never recovered from that.

And how difficult was it for you as a diplomat trying to negotiate, when you had, on one hand, the public pressure in the United States with the Left saying, "Get out now at any price, any cost, just go," and on the other hand the North Vietnamese and Le Duc Tho exploiting that?

It was maddening to be accused of not having made offers which we knew we had already put on the table. There were always articles that alleged that we should do just one more little thing when most of the time, we had already done it. In any event, there was really only one issue: are we willing to overthrow a government which our predecessors had put into office to permit a Vietnamese society to be free, or as free as we could make it, and replace it by imposing a communist government? This would have been a violation of everything America stood for in the post–World War II period. It would have been an act of total cynicism.

SEVEN

Breakthrough and the Paris Accords

The final agreement exceeded expectations and the calls of many critics. Ever since, two stubborn shibboleths have persisted: This pact was overdue because Nixon and Kissinger could have made it much earlier. This pact was cynical because Nixon and Kissinger knew it would fail after a "decent interval."

In other words, they should have made a deal earlier that they should never have made at all.

These are the facts: From day one, the North Vietnamese ruled out the contours of the final agreement and then concrete offers; they insisted that we overthrow the Saigon government while we withdrew our forces. Finally, in the fall of 1972, facing the prospect of four more years of Nixon, they dropped their political demands and agreed to the original American proposal for a military settlement only.

While harboring no illusions about our adversary's goals, we believed the Paris Accords could be sustained through enforcement of the cease-fire, assistance to Saigon, economic incentives for Hanoi, and the self-interested support of Beijing and Moscow.

Nixon and Kissinger were convinced that these factors would give the South Vietnamese a "decent opportunity" to shape their own future so long as the United States upheld its responsibilities. Because the United States reneged on its pledges, we will never know whether our ally could have seized this reasonable chance.

* * *

So what changed from the beginning of 1972 to the end of 1972, when the North Vietnamese came around? What caused them to do that?

At the beginning of 1972, Hanoi started an all-out offensive against South Vietnam, moving practically their entire army into South Vietnam. By that time, we had withdrawn our combat forces. We really only had air and naval power left. So the South Vietnamese had to resist that offensive by using only South Vietnamese forces. This was a test, therefore, of Vietnamization. Nixon introduced substantial additional air power, primarily B-52s. The combination of these two trends defeated the North Vietnamese offensive and, in fact, damaged the North Vietnamese to a point where some territory that had been lost earlier in the war was recovered.

So when they accepted our January proposal in October, our judgment was that they were weakened significantly, that they could not defeat South Vietnam except with all-out force, and that we would resist that as allies. We would help the South Vietnamese, in the case of an all-out attack, but, on the whole, the major thrust of the South Vietnamese defense had to be in South Vietnamese hands.

When we made the breakthrough in October, it seemed to us they were reading the election prospects of Nixon getting re-elected and [George] McGovern not winning, and they're going to get this madman for another four years.

To understand the Paris Accords, one has to consider the sequence by which we reached those terms. Very early in the Nixon Administration, we decided on the policy of gradual withdrawal, building up the Vietnamese forces, and emerging at the end with an agreement in which American forces would be totally withdrawn. The Vietnamese would be able to undertake their own defense except in the case of an all-out attack. So the evolution of the negotiations had been that we gradually reduced the interval between the agreement and the time of our withdrawal in line with the number of troops we had already withdrawn and our judgment of South Vietnamese capabilities.

And so these terms constantly kept shrinking. We started out with a deadline of sixteen months and, by 1972, we had the withdrawal period down to two months. The one fundamental condition on which we never yielded was that the people of Vietnam must have an opportunity to determine their own fate.

There were various occasions where we thought we were close to an agreement. In effect, we had settled many of the subsidiary points, except the one on the political structure of South Vietnam. Then, as I said, in October 1972, after the failure of their all-out offensive, which was defeated by South Vietnamese ground forces and American air power, Le Duc Tho, at a session on October 6, 1972, said he had a new proposal. The new proposal in effect accepted a public proposal that Nixon had made in the previous January, in which the continuation of the Saigon administration was agreed to, South Vietnam was treated as a political entity for the peacetime period, and the United States would withdraw in that context. That was the fundamental breakthrough.

After that, there were days of intense negotiation of many fine points of the agreement, on many of which the North Vietnamese yielded because at that point we had won the ground war in the sense that there was no prospect of the North Vietnamese defeating the Saigon government with the forces they had in the country. We were aware that maintaining an agreement would be complicated, because South Vietnam has really long borders, and to control infiltration would always be difficult. In essence, we were convinced that the agreement would enable the South Vietnamese, whose political survival we had assured, to also maintain their security position in the future.

Also, as Winston said, the North Vietnamese knew that they would have to deal with Nixon for another four years, and he had demonstrated at every key point that he would not permit a defeat.

So their attitude changed for two reasons: One, because they were defeated on the battlefield. And also because they recognized that Nixon was going to be reelected.

They were very eager to settle the war before Nixon's reelection, because they thought that afterwards, the pattern of the previous four years might be repeated. On the other hand, we were under pressure to conclude because we knew that a Democratic Congress would come in despite Nixon's likely reelection, and that the dominant theme of the Congress was to cut off appropriations for Vietnam.

In any event, we got the final accord, which was much better than most critics thought was possible. Could you outline the elements of that accord?

The proposals we had put forward that were the essence of the final settlement were ridiculed by the media as being unattainable and a demonstration of Nixon's commitment to war. In fact, we got terms better than thought possible because of the negotiating process that I've described. The differences between what we put forward in May 1971 and what we achieved were mostly technical in nature.

Hanoi yielded on the key point that the Saigon government could remain in office, and that the Saigon government would not have to be modified as a result of the negotiation. And that whatever modifications would take place would be the result of the will of the Vietnamese people. But the existing government would stay in office and would be a principal party to the enforcement of the agreement. That was the key concession.

The fall of 1972 was the first time we had an analytical advantage. Before then, Hanoi had correctly assessed that the lack of endurance of the American people would drive us out of the war. So for four years they had really conducted the negotiations just to procrastinate the war until they could then give it a final push with their offensive.

Then America showed more determination than they had expected. They suddenly became panicked about what would happen if Nixon got reelected. So starting about the beginning of September, they became very anxious to agree on a schedule to end the war, when before that their pressure had been exactly the opposite. We had an advantage in that sense, that they were terrified of a Nixon reelection. But we knew that even if he got reelected, he would lose the Congress, as all the polls showed he would do, and Congress would vote us out of the war no matter what happened. So we and they converged on trying to end it before the election. But Nixon's electoral advantage was so great at the time that it was totally unnecessary for domestic reasons.

And also, he wouldn't make an imperfect agreement just to get reelected. Moreover, he didn't need it.

Yes, because the criticism was that Nixon would have agreed to anything in order to get reelected.

Yes.

First of all, Nixon didn't bother with the details. He didn't send detailed instructions during the negotiations. When the agreement was completed, we told the North Vietnamese it now had to go to Nixon for approval, which he gave. But he had approved the outline of it when we started. That's the way Nixon and I worked together, that we would agree on the principles, but he wouldn't second-guess every move along the way. Then at the end of it, of course, he would exercise the presidential role of final approval.

What we got in this negotiation, we had been told by the peace movement for two years, was unattainable. Look at the record. We did not make any significant concessions in the final negotiations.

So, by October of 1972, you had achieved your objectives in the negotiations. What were the main characteristics of the Paris Accords? Why did you think the agreement would succeed, and why do you think it ultimately didn't succeed?

Yes. We thought that we had achieved the key objectives. Remember I pointed out that we had already more or less settled the rate of American withdrawal. But the key objective over which all previous negotiations had failed was Hanoi's insistence that before any peace process could start, before they would even talk about the release of American prisoners, the Saigon government had to be overthrown. The overthrow of the Saigon government was the condition that took precedence over all other terms for Hanoi's negotiators. And this was reversed by their October concessions.

So when you had an agreement that was finalized, you had some confidence that it could succeed.

Let me explain what the key terms of the January 1973 agreement were. There was a cease-fire. There was a prohibition of infiltration, and the only new equipment that could be introduced into South Vietnam would be replacement of damaged or destroyed existing weapons. A UN inspection system would supervise compliance. So the balance could not be overturned except by illegal infiltration.

So we were convinced, as a result of these provisions, that the South Vietnamese would be able to resist whatever military forces would be left in the country. And that we would help them in case of an all-out attack, which would mean a total violation of all the key provisions.

There was also international machinery established to check that the introduction of new equipment into Vietnam could occur only through authorized United Nations checkpoints. These provisions applied to both sides. Simultaneously, we agreed to the principle that the United States would extend some economic aid to North Vietnam, which we conceived as a means of controlling the execution of the agreement. In fact, Nixon sent me to Hanoi in February 1973 in part to negotiate some details of this economic package.

This aid was also extended to South Vietnam, Laos, and Cambodia.

Yes. All the provisions of the agreement applied also to Laos and Cambodia. Now the North Vietnamese took the position that the communist forces in Laos and Cambodia were autonomous and that they could not always guarantee that they would execute the preferences of Hanoi. We found out later this was probably true for Cambodia but was certainly not true for Laos.

Also, this economic provision was seen as an incentive to the Hanoi Politburo to opt for reconstruction of their economy as opposed to violating the agreement. And we hoped that this, together with the other factors—for example, the Chinese and Russians having an interest in restraining the North Vietnamese: American support—would preserve the agreement.

In addition, we had enough experience by now to realize that the tensions between China and the Soviet Union were quite severe. And that China certainly was not interested in another military operation in Indochina. So we thought all these factors together created a plausible outcome in which we could achieve our fundamental objective of ending a war, which three American administrations of both parties had conducted, by having given an allied government that had relied on us every opportunity to survive. That was our principal objective.

There's been criticism of the agreement because of tapes which would come out saying that you wanted a "decent interval." Could you explain what that means?

First of all, one has to keep in mind that there are multiple records of so many conversations, and when these conversations are then made public, it is never made clear in what context they were taken. There were some conversations with the Chinese, there were conversations with my staff, there were conversations with Nixon. A fundamental theme that concerned us was this: will the United States be obliged for the indefinite future to defend South Vietnam no matter how corrupt its government, or how inefficient its administration?

Our view was we wanted to give the South Vietnamese a decent opportunity to survive. We never defined exactly what we meant by "decent." But we certainly didn't mean it as a subterfuge by which we could pull out, and the North Vietnamese would then defeat the South, and our hands were clean. We meant a genuine opportunity to survive by helping them to build up an adequate army and by supporting them economically. We had in mind something like how South Korea evolved after the Korean War.

Now, we never addressed formally how many years, but we surely weren't sitting around saying, "Let's come up with an agreement that they can easily overthrow, and we'll fool the American public." By "decent" we meant what the word "decent" means: something that we could believe ourselves and could tell the American people—that we gave South Vietnam a genuine opportunity. We thought we had achieved that, but it is often presented as if it were some sort of trickery. We went through years of war for what we considered the honor of American foreign policy and the cause of freedom. More than Vietnam was involved.

When you look around the world in '69, the Soviet Union had just occupied Czechoslovakia, then they had moved forty-plus divisions to the borders of China. We feared an imminent assault on China, which might have overturned the international equilibrium. We wanted an agreement that would maintain our credibility in becoming the linchpin of the international peace system.

But then what went wrong? You had given the North Vietnamese incentives to abide by the agreement, as well as the South Vietnamese, Laos, and Cambodia.

It's a national tragedy, which we have not yet overcome. When I was a graduate student in the fifties, Harvard was 90 percent Democratic, as it has remained and maybe increased, but when Republican Cabinet members showed up at Harvard, they were treated with respect. The political debate in America in the fifties and early sixties was about the adequacy of policies. Sometime in the sixties, the political debate turned into a debate about the motivation of leaders and their inherent moral adequacy.

And it became fashionable to accuse presidents and Cabinet members of representing immoral systems against which any kind of violent demonstration was not only permitted but necessary. So this tendency of trying to squelch opposing views became a dominant view. President Johnson could not make public appearances. He had to speak only at army bases in order to fulfill the security requirements of the Secret Service. So the fundamental domestic problem we had in negotiating was that we could not generate a debate in which people dealt with the war in terms of substantive issues. Nixon in the public debate then replaced Johnson as the villain who wanted the war, who continued the war.

In fact, if you look at the actual documents, you will see that the Nixon Administration accepted practically all of the proposals that led to the sharp divisions in the Democratic Party in 1968. We more or less adopted much of the peace platform that [presidential candidate Hubert] Humphrey had at the Democratic Convention of 1968. In 1968, the Democrats were not in favor of unilateral withdrawal. But step by step, the demands of the opposition in the United States were raised to the point where at the end, all they asked for America to withdraw unilaterally was the release of our prisoners.

But to end the war simply by getting a release of your own prisoners would be to make a travesty of what had gone on, starting in the Truman Administration, reinforced in the Kennedy Administration, accelerated in the Johnson Administration, and continued by Nixon.

Plus the critics not only wanted unilateral withdrawal for prisoners, but also in effect to overthrow the Saigon government as we left.

Yes. So when we got an agreement that exceeded expectations, we thought there would be support in the Congress for maintaining it. We don't know whether that would have been possible or not. But then Watergate so undermined presidential authority that the radical view in Congress became ascendant. The agreement was formalized in January 1973. And by June, it was apparent that there were gross violations on the part of the North Vietnamese. We asked Le Duc Tho to meet us again in Paris to review all these violations. But in the interval [from January to June 1973] the Congress had passed a set of provisions that prohibited the use of American military force in, over, or near Indochina.

So we lost the capacity to enforce the agreement. In addition, there was a systematic assault on the appropriations for assistance, so that the South Vietnamese side never produced as vital a government as one would have expected given the conditions at the end of '72. The Congress voted us out of the war basically when it prohibited the use of any American forces in, over, or near Vietnam, and cut off all aid to Cambodia. That was the end of it.

They not only cut off chances of bombing, for example, but they even cut off military aid.

They cut off military aid to Cambodia altogether, and they sharply reduced military aid to Saigon. And by 1974, they came up with ideas for a terminal package. There had been a tacit agreement between Senator [John C.] Stennis [chairman of the Senate Armed Services Committee] and President Nixon that the Congress in 1975 would pass a supplementary budget which would make up deficiencies in the previous appropriations. But by 1975, Nixon had resigned and, in effect, the Congress refused to pass this appropriation. So the South Vietnamese had to ration ammunition in the defense against the last assault.

So at the end, we really reneged on the terms of the agreement. Is that how you saw it?

Congress put us in a position where we could not execute it.

And whatever the weaknesses of the South Vietnamese army, the psychological blow of not getting any military aid, not to mention the material blow, was pretty crucial.

The idea of conducting foreign policy on behalf of American credibility is now conventionally ridiculed. But it was one of the key elements of the Vietnamese war, because potential allies, actual allies, threatened countries were bound to assess their future in terms of the American performance in Vietnam.

While you were trying to maintain the peace agreement with Vietnam, Congress took its own actions. How did that have an impact elsewhere?

Well, countries that were covered by an American guarantee or alliance thought that they had to discount the American pledges. And forces within countries that thought of overthrowing the existing institutions, which they thought had been protected by American alliances and friendship, were bolder in launching their pressures.

EIGHT

Initial Advances
in the Middle East

Often there are improbable assets gleaned from crises. As President Nixon once observed, the same Chinese character denotes both "crisis" and "opportunity."

So it was with the October 1973 Yom Kippur War. It erupted against the background of twenty-five years of hostility between Tel Aviv and Cairo, and Arab reliance on Soviet arms. When Egypt made significant advances and then Israel reversed the tide, threatening to wipe out Egyptian forces, Kissinger grasped an opportunity for diplomacy.

He moved immediately to freeze the battlefield through a cease-fire at a delicate stage where Israel was sobered by its initial setbacks, and Egypt felt it had gained respect. Both sides were ready to negotiate. The United States demonstrated that only Washington mediation, and not Soviet arms, could yield progress.

As Kissinger wrote in *A World Restored,* one can sometimes "chart a course through tempestuous waters, where the violence of the elements imparts inspiration through the need for survival."

* * *

How did this affect things in the Middle East? As you turned from Vietnam to the Middle East, what was the impact on the 1973 Arab-Israeli war for American credibility, for allies and adversaries?

Well, I would argue that the willingness of countries to start a war in the Middle East certainly included the calculation that the United States might not be in a position to defend its traditional allies.

As you were dealing with Vietnam, the Soviet Union, arms control agreements, and China in the first several years of the Nixon Administration, you didn't seem to focus much on the Middle East. Why was that?

First, I was security advisor and not secretary of state, and my priorities were, importantly, assigned by President Nixon. President Nixon in those years thought that he would let the State Department handle the Middle East, because he thought that whatever progress could be made would depend on conventional negotiations and did not require constant presidential involvement. So in the first few years, we monitored the negotiations from the White House and intervened on certain key issues. But we did not actually conduct the negotiations out of the White House.

What changed with the October 1973 war? Why did Nixon and you feel there might be an opportunity for diplomacy?

We always had the view that the breakthrough in negotiations would come when one of the Arab countries concluded that Soviet military support was not the way to achieve their objectives. In '69, I gave a press conference in which I said it was our intention to expel Russian military presence from the Middle East. It was unwise to announce, but that was our strategy. In fact, Nixon was willing to wait four years before he could do it.

To briefly sketch the situation as it was in the early years of the Nixon Administration: All the key Arab countries, except Jordan and Saudi Arabia, were either explicit or indirect allies of the Soviet Union. All of the countries bordering Israel were getting their key military equipment from the Soviet Union. They and the Soviet Union voted together in the UN. So we did not think there could be any progress in negotiations until some major Arab country split from this lineup. Saudi Arabia was a permanent friend of the United States, but on its own ideologically and very hostile to Israel.

So this was the lineup. We thought that when the war started, it was an opportunity to convince the Arab world that America could be a major factor in the peace settlement. We had had some indications of it before that when [Egyptian president Anwar] Sadat sent his national security advisor to Washington to begin exploring discussions between the United States and Egypt. But that mission occurred just before the American and Israeli elections, so we deferred the quest for a breakthrough until after the elections.

But we were actually conducting those conversations with the expectations that late in '73 there might be a diplomatic breakthrough. So when, instead, Egypt and Syria attacked Israel, we decided to use that as the opportunity to try to make the breakthrough. At the very beginning of the war, our judgment—not so much Nixon's and mine alone but the CIA and the military's—we all thought that the Arab side would suffer a crushing defeat, and that very quickly the Israeli military would be deep in Egypt and Syria. So we proposed on the first day of the war a return to the status quo ante and a cease-fire, which was a way to demonstrate that the United States wanted a settlement to start with the status quo.

As it happened, the Egyptian and Syrian surprise attack gained some substantial territory, so that the negotiating pattern had changed. But we were in almost daily communication with Egypt, warning them with the following theme: "You're making war with Soviet arms. Keep in mind that you will have to make peace with American diplomacy." And so we did not see in this war what had happened in the '67 war: mass demonstrations in the Arab capitals against America. On the contrary, a mission of Arab foreign ministers came to Washington right after the war.

During the war, we managed to establish ourselves as mediators between the Arab and the Israeli sides, never raising the slightest doubt that we would not permit an Israeli military defeat, but also making it clear that as soon as the war was over, we would lead a diplomatic initiative to bring about a solution. And we were lucky that our counterpart, on the Egyptian side at least, was President Sadat, who was one of the great men whom I have met in my experience in government. But Sadat had to move very carefully to make clear his decision to rely on American diplomacy. So the war had to be ended before the peace process could start, and we had to do this in conjunction with the Soviet Union, because the Soviet Union still had the major influence in the Arab world. I took a trip to Moscow to negotiate this, which had its own dramatic aspects.

I went to Moscow when the Israelis had crossed the Suez Canal, and they had destroyed the air defense system that the Soviets had built along the Suez Canal, and they could move almost freely. They were also gaining ground in Syria. So at that point, the Soviets were eager to get a cease-fire. Our challenge was that just defeating the Arab armies would not get us to a peace settlement. So at any rate, while I was in Russia, Nixon sent a telegram to Brezhnev saying that Kissinger has full powers to bring this war to a conclusion.

The first evening there, I was invited to see Brezhnev at midnight and he said, "I'm eager to settle." I said, "Well, but you understand I have to keep checking everything with Nixon." And he pulled out a cable from Nixon sent without my knowledge, and he said, "No, you have full authority, Nixon communicated to me." I was outraged to be deprived of maneuvering room, because I wanted to gain time by invoking the need to check back with Nixon, because time was working for us. So I called [Nixon's chief of staff, General Alexander] Haig and said, "Are you crazy? What are you doing?" And he said, "I have problems of my own." And I said, "What problems could you possibly have on a Saturday night in Washington?" He told me that it was the night of the "Saturday night massacre," where the attorney general and several others had been fired as a result of Watergate.

So Watergate had crucially weakened us. But the agreement we made the next day was a cease-fire and the beginning of a direct negotiation between Egypt and Israel, which all Arab states had refused for twenty years.

When Sadat sent his security advisor to Washington the year before to explore improving U.S.-Egyptian relations, did you and Nixon have an inkling then that there might be a role that American diplomacy could play?

Yes. But we wanted to get the American and Israeli elections behind us. This is an occasion for amusing anecdotes: at the end of the Egyptian national security advisor's [Hafiz Ismail's] presentation in the meeting with me, he said, "If these negotiations make progress, President Sadat may invite you to Cairo." I wrote a little note to [national security assistant] Peter Rodman sitting next to me saying, "Would it be impolite to ask him what the second prize is?"

Getting back to the cease-fire, isn't it fair to say that by getting this achieved before the Israelis would have really wiped out the Egyptian army, the Egyptians had enough self-confidence that they had not been humiliated, and Israeli's early losses sobered them up a little bit? So both were ready to make some moves?

Well, the front line was like this: The Egyptian Second Army had crossed the Suez Canal, but the Israelis had gotten behind them in crossing the Suez Canal. And they had practically trapped them. So if the war had continued, the Second Army would have been wiped out. Sadat would have been overthrown, and another radical regime would have taken power in Cairo. We thought that this was an opportunity where, by permitting a negotiation about the future of the Second Army, we gave both sides an occasion to give content to the American diplomatic mediation. There was thus a military contact also that they agreed to undertake. And this for a while was cause for a big domestic debate in the U.S. But the evolution then led in the next years to two major agreements with Egypt, a disengagement agreement with Syria, and eventually a peace agreement, which is still the element of stability for the whole Middle East.

Before the Arabs mounted their attack on Israel in October of 1973, did the United States have any advance warning that this was happening? Did our intelligence pick up anything about the Arabs preparing a surprise attack?

No. In the week before, I was confirmed as secretary of state. In my first weekend, I went into the State Department to see what the State Department intelligence system had produced. They told me that there were Arab concentrations on the Syrian front and some movement on the Suez Canal. So I asked all the agencies—the Pentagon and the CIA—for their information. They all agreed that these were maneuvers, that they did not signify imminent hostilities. I asked them for a report every forty-eight hours, and it was not until twenty-four hours before the attack that people began getting nervous that it might be the prelude to an attack and not just a demonstration.

Did you warn the Israelis?

Well, every time we asked one of the American agencies, we also informed the Israelis. And the Israelis and the American intelligence were working so closely together that we received essentially the same intelligence reports—that those moves were not preparations for war but a kind of military exercise. In the previous years, we had had so much experience with Arab troop movements that turned out to be just bluff that this must have affected the thinking of all the intelligence analysts who made these reports.

So twenty-four hours before, when you thought it might be an attack, did the Israelis give any consideration about a preemptive attack as they had done in the 1967 war?

Well, they may have given consideration internally, but they did not ask us about preemption. Our view would have been, had they asked us, to warn them against preemption.

Why?

Because we did not want them to be considered the aggressor in a Middle East war. Having just gone through the Vietnam experience in our country, we thought paying attention to the domestic situation was very important. But this never became an actual issue. The Israelis never asked us whether we would object to a preemptive war, or never told us that they intended to launch a preemptive attack. This was Yom Kippur, when most of the Israelis who were not needed for extreme security measures were in synagogues. We never received even the hint of a request to launch a preemptive attack. The time limit was very short.

The war started on Saturday morning American time. It was not until Friday afternoon that there was any beginning consideration that this might actually turn into an attack. And starting Saturday morning, we got in touch with all the countries involved. In our first intergovernmental exchange on it, the intelligence estimate still was that this was a war probably started by Israel. It was not clear at the beginning what was happening.

In any event, when you achieved the cease-fire, you set up the stage for shuttle negotiations in which you and the president could be defending Israel at all times, but as honest brokers, not just as an advocate for Israel; you could deal with both sides.

Well, we had a basic premise that we would do nothing that the Israelis thought would affect their security. But we were also determined to initiate a diplomatic process which would overcome, first of all, the Arab refusal to talk to Israel directly, and in which both Egyptians and Syrians would be prepared to negotiate not only a cease-fire but a realignment, a disengagement of forces.

So did you help shape the cease-fire while you were in Moscow talking with the Russians? Did you get their agreement?

No. We drafted the outlines of a cease-fire but, remember, this required being in contact with the White House a number of times a day. We had all along told the Israelis that if there were a proposal for a cease-fire, we would do our utmost to support it. So we knew the general conditions. There was some argument that we should have let them destroy the Second Army. Our judgment was that it would have finished any progress toward peace. And one has to compare where Egypt and Israel stand now in relation to each other compared to what would have been the case if a radical kind of regime would have emerged in Cairo.

So at the end of that war and while you are helping negotiate the cease-fire, did you comprehend that there might have opened a real opportunity for Arab-Israeli negotiations, even Arab-Israeli peace? Because it seemed to happen very quickly.

That was the basis of our diplomacy. The condition in which the cease-fire was established was that Arab and Israeli negotiators would meet at a point along the road from Suez toward Israel. One of the time-exhausting things was that there was a different perception where that marker was. So there was a few hours' delay in defining where that marker was. But at any rate, there were two levels of cease-fire. There was the cease-fire that was established on the basis of my trip to Moscow, which was supposed to end the immediate conflict. That was put through the Security Council. That established a legal framework.

But then the question was, all right, there's the cease-fire. But what are the dividing lines? That was finally achieved through a negotiation between Egyptians and Israelis at a designated point along a road that went from Egypt to Palestine.

How did you get both sides to trust you—you Kissinger, you Nixon, you the United States—to be the honest broker?

And how soon did the shuttle negotiations get launched?

The first issue was the cease-fire and the dividing line. The sequence was like this. There was a UN draft for the cease-fire that was initially negotiated by Brezhnev and me with the approval of Nixon that had to be put through the Security Council. After that was established, then a debate followed—where is the dividing line? Because the Israelis had continued their offensive and pursued it really until they had completely trapped the Second Army, which was not actually fully trapped at the moment the cease-fire was passed.

So they took a few more hours to take advantage before the cease-fire was agreed on?

They took a day or so more to keep going. So then we insisted that the cease-fire be observed. This took about a week after the negotiation in Moscow. I think the negotiation in Moscow was on a Sunday, and the final agreement that Egyptian and Israeli negotiators would meet on Kilometer 101 was on Friday night. But I could be wrong by twenty-four hours, something like that. After that, we initiated a new diplomacy, which said that now that there is a cease-fire line, let us see whether we can negotiate a disengagement of forces. The Israelis would withdraw some distance from the Suez Canal and, in effect, a demilitarized zone would be established between the two sides.

At that point, I went to the Middle East to sell the details of this concept. And in order to get it completed, since it depended on where the lines would be, we started the shuttle diplomacy. But you have to remember when we talk about my activities, I would write a daily lengthy report to Nixon of where we stood in the negotiation.

So he was actively engaged in the negotiations throughout this, despite the Watergate crisis?

Well, Nixon was actively engaged in reviewing the evolving positions.

A further point on the '73 Middle East war: There's a little book that a participant in the Soviet decision-making process wrote about their daily meetings. And you can see in that book that the Soviets were torn. On the one hand, they wanted to do their revolutionary duty to allies; but on the other, they wanted to maintain their relationship with the United States.

And so, in fact, they never acted with the crispness that we did, because we had a strategy we had talked about for years and full presidential backing. Our strategy was to thwart any initiative supported by Soviet arms, to teach the region what we later expressed in a sentence. "You can make war with Soviet arms, but you can make peace only with American diplomacy." Our strategy was that when we had taught that lesson, and some Arab country decided to rely on American diplomacy, we would act quickly and decisively. We knew that between ourselves for years. We never had the chance until Sadat decided to change course, but we built up to it. We took a very tough stance in the Jordanian civil war in 1970. We took a very tough stance at the opening phase of the '73 war. We always remained in touch with potential adversaries. We never tried to put ourselves in a position where we would be standing there naked, vulnerable to everybody, while we pursued one particular course. That was hard to teach into a bureaucratic framework. But the people who worked with me for years, they did it more or less automatically by that time.

Now, the first shuttle was fairly quick, maybe ten days. The first shuttle established an Israeli withdrawal from the Suez Canal of, I forget, fifteen miles, something like that. But it was the first retreat by Israel from territories occupied in the 1967 war. And it established principles by which the two countries could interact afterwards. It put limitations on the number of forces they could have along the dividing line. It was an important step toward peace, and it provided for another negotiation that took place a year and a half later, for a further Israeli withdrawal in return for an end of many of the political measures that had been taken on the Arab side. So it was the beginning of the end of belligerency.

Talk to us about that intervening year and a half, the relationship that the United States started developing with Sadat and Egypt.

Well, in that year and a half, Nixon left office for one thing, and Egypt became the key country of our diplomacy. But in order to create a general condition of peace, we then

negotiated a comparable disengagement agreement between Israel and Syria. And that took a thirty-plus-day
shuttle to get established. That still exists to this day. Even
the ISIS people in Syria have observed that limitation.

*And so that's how shuttle diplomacy has become associated
with Henry Kissinger.*

NINE

Negotiating Styles and Personal Profiles

If history is the memory of states, negotiating styles are often the product of history.

In dealing with diverse personalities, Kissinger found their techniques often reflected the historical psyches of their countries: a confident nation, with a glorious history, taking the long view. A paranoid nation, subject to invasions, haggling like rug merchants. A revolutionary nation, allergic to compromise, wielding talks as a weapon. A wary nation, surrounded by hostility, examining texts with Talmudic fervor.

In handling these distinct styles, Kissinger employed different mixes of history and projection, firmness and inducement, patience and urgency, aggravation and humor. But throughout, he adhered to two fundamental principles—early exposition of America's fundamental goals and constant attention to his interlocutor's international posture and domestic realities.

* * *

I think we'd like to go now to diplomacy. What key principles would you leave to leaders today of how to conduct diplomacy? You've given us examples of you and Nixon looking several steps ahead of things you wanted to prevent from happening or encourage to happen, but what would be some other key principles?

Including negotiations.

We didn't enter government with a precise theory of negotiations, but I would say the following: One, we always began every diplomatic effort with a question: "What are we trying to do here? What is the purpose of this exercise?" So we tried never to be obsessed with all the technical details of a negotiation. We always sought to focus on where we were trying to come out. We tried to lay down certain principles for ourselves and wrote many papers to ourselves of what we were trying to do here and reviewed them. This was true with Vietnam, where we early on developed the strategy of separating the political from the military issues, and emphasized that the political issues should be solved by the Vietnamese, while we would address the military issues.

And leaving aside the merit, it pretty well wound up that way and the agreement reflected that design. We then didn't maintain the agreement because of our domestic upheavals.

The same process was true with China. In general, I would say that the Nixon foreign policy began with the question "Where are we trying to go?," not in just a formal sense but in a very explicit sense.

So it was far more than just the process, it was the end state that was the goal?

Yes. What's the end state? We never believed that negotiations by themselves would generate magically some outcome. We thought the process of negotiations would support what we were trying to achieve. You could apply that, I would say, to every negotiation that we conducted. We strove to enter negotiations by knowing what we thought the outcome should be and how it should be reached. The result of that attitude was that we made serious efforts to understand the thinking of the other side, so that we did not go in with a fixed notion of a permanent enemy as an abstract. So we tried to understand what the other side was trying to accomplish because, at the end of a negotiation, you must have parties that are willing to support it. Otherwise, you're just negotiating an armistice. When we encountered irreconcilable hostility or unbridgeable conflict, we strove for a strategy to overcome it.

Then I had views on the practice of negotiating. The conventional approach to negotiations is to state your maximum objective, and then slice away at it and give up a little bit at a time until you come to a final conclusion.

I've always objected to that on the ground that when you engage in these so-called salami tactics, you never know when you have reached the end, and everything becomes a test of strength and endurance. So my general approach, and I say "mine" because I was the practical negotiator for much of this, was to offer very quickly the basic objective, the basic goals we were trying to reach, maybe plus 5 percent, and then explain it to the other side at great lengths. The purpose was to probe for a conceptual understanding.

Winston was present for almost all of it, so he may confirm that I usually spent a lot of time in explaining our long-range goals strategically and philosophically. I thought the other side would have to make its decisions on the basis of some assessment of their aims, and they needed to hear ours.

And I would say the negotiations that succeeded occurred when the other side gave you a comparably frank explanation. I would say negotiations with Zhou Enlai and Sadat were examples of that, where we were not bargaining about little items, where we were making big jumps toward a defined objective.

Wouldn't you contrast that with the Russian rug merchant style, or the Vietnamese, where negotiating was an act of war, in effect?

Absolutely. This did not work with the Vietnamese as a method, because the Vietnamese were not interested in the solution; they were interested in a victory, and therefore they looked at the negotiations as a way to undermine our morale.

And the negotiations were protracted because we would not leave our position and nor would they until the very end. There came that magic day where they handed us a piece of paper which, in effect, was their acceptance of a proposal that Nixon had made publicly eight months earlier. And, as I said, at the end of that session I shook hands with Winston and said, "We've done it!" That turned out to be wrong.

I would say premature, not wrong.

Well, it was premature. The agreement did happen, three months later, but it wasn't maintained, because after Watergate there was no support for enforcing the agreement.

Henry, how did you reconcile your approach to negotiations with the Russian approach? How did you manage to square that? Because they obviously were not like the Chinese or Sadat.

Well, Sadat and the Chinese each made a decision to change the framework within which they were operating, Sadat because he understood that he could not achieve his aims by military means. You might say, "Well, but he went to war," but he went to war just to establish himself as a serious negotiator. He did not think that the war would be in itself decisive.

And the Chinese were concerned about a Soviet attack, and they wanted to add as much power to their side as they could.

The Russians did not yet have a view compatible to ours when we began negotiations. The Russians were dealing with us as permanent adversaries. But in the course of these evolutions with the Russians there emerged, I don't want to say the realization, but a kind of conviction, that the Cold War needed to be ended in some fashion. We had not yet reached agreement exactly on how to do this, and in the absence of that agreement the Russian negotiating method was the retail business. They sold every item several times!

And one last example: the Israelis, given their insecurities in history, were pretty meticulous in going over details.

The Israeli problem was that the margin of survival was so narrow, and the gap between what would threaten our survival and theirs so wide, that they had to demonstrate that every item they gave up had to be purchased by at least the psychological exhaustion of their negotiating partner. So every Israeli negotiation went to the last minute, of the last hour, of the last day, so that they could prove to themselves that they could not have extracted any more than they had. But while it was nerve-racking to deal with, I had great sympathy for Israel because when you looked at the relationship of populations, and when you're in Israel and you can drive across the whole country in an hour, giving up territory has a different significance than for a continental country.

In what you just described to us, negotiating with the Russians in this way, the Israelis in that way, and then Sadat and China, how much is it a national characteristic, and how much of it is the quality of the leaders that you were negotiating with?

Well, our national characteristic is not to negotiate the historic and strategic way the Nixon Administration did. Our national characteristic is to think that diplomats enter the fray when there is a problem, and that you can solve the problem by a legal and meticulous type of negotiating one issue at a time, and we've been able to do this because we have two great oceans behind which to operate.

In a way, each nation's negotiating style is partly the result of its historical circumstance. The Russians are so detailed in their negotiations and so aggressive in their tactics, because they're living on a territory that's been invaded from all sides for hundreds of years, and therefore their confidence in the reliability of surrounding countries is extremely, extremely limited. The same is true to some extent of Israel.

The Arab societies have been torn between their missionary impulses, which reflect a great deal of their history, and the realities of the environment in which they operate. So during the period of the Nixon Administration, the Arab states were acting as national states, but there was always an undercurrent of missionary fervor that might suddenly erupt.

It seems to me that the Chinese with their "Middle Kingdom" complex had a certain self-confidence that allowed them to take the long view. Wouldn't you say that induced them to back our diplomatic approach?

The Chinese don't think of negotiations as solving individual problems. The Chinese think that every solution is an admission ticket for another problem. So they think in terms of processes.

And one of the problems American and Chinese negotiators have with each other is the Americans usually have some specific items they want to achieve, while the Chinese want to know where do we think we are going and what are we willing to do in an historic process.

For Nixon, which is almost unprecedented in American diplomatic history, he went to China to spend days with Zhou Enlai discussing strategic views. No American president I encountered or studied would have been willing to spend so much effort on creating a philosophic framework.

You had negotiated with Zhou Enlai several times on the secret trip and subsequent trips, spending hours talking to him about big-picture things. How was it different working with Zhou Enlai and then with Mao? What was it in their approaches that was different?

Zhou Enlai was a man of great intellectual brilliance and great personal charm. And he negotiated in the framework of extraordinary knowledge, extraordinary patience, and without any attempt to assert a relative balance of forces. There were occasions when he was very tough, but he negotiated in those phases in a persuasive framework, that we were two serious people who had decided to go in a certain direction, and we would try to find the best means of achieving it. So he would pick up little things—if somebody in our group was ill, or had any previous connection—and would always find a way to make a reference to it. But he never tried to ingratiate himself personally.

Mao was the incarnation of revolutionary dedication. Mao exuded dominance. Like a great actor on the stage, he seized the audience in the first thirty seconds. Mao did not try to persuade you particularly, he stated dicta. He would almost invariably begin a conversation with a question. Unlike most statesmen, he didn't say, "I have five points to make." He would say, "What is your consideration of . . . ?" Then he would take you to the next step and answer it by means of a Socratic dialogue, however interrupted at various stages by cynical comments, which would convey, "Don't try to fool this expert in human frailty."

One of his classic rejoinders was, "You Americans remind me of swallows who fly up into the air at an approaching storm and flap your wings. But you, professor, and I know that the flapping of the wings does not affect the coming of the storm." Or you would tell him about some negotiation, and he just threw in "Munich." . . . But this was all done with great courtesy. He exuded the conviction that he knew where the world was going, and you had to fit into that scheme.

We had one meeting of about three hours on a trip after the Nixon-Mao summit. He made a review of the entire world. He covered in detail even countries like Oman, Pakistan, and we really didn't know the purpose of the exercise. David Bruce, who was our representative in Beijing at the time, said it was the most extraordinary performance he had seen. And he had known leaders like [French President Charles] de Gaulle and [German Chancellor Konrad] Adenauer. It was only clear later on when Zhou Enlai was in effect removed from office that our meeting was an opportunity for Mao to work out his directives and concepts. And after that, no Chinese leader ever mentioned Zhou Enlai again. When they referred to any higher authority, they referred to a Mao text or transcript.

Isn't it fair to say that in the Nixon-Mao meeting, Nixon wanted to talk about substance, and Mao kept saying that's up to the premier. And we were a little taken aback by the brief comments that Mao made on each issue. But as the days went on, we realized these were his brushstrokes for setting up a strategic context.

There was another thing. I have since talked to Nancy Tang, who was his interpreter at the time. We did not know that the week before Nixon arrived Mao had fallen very ill and that there was serious consideration to cancel the trip, but enormous reluctance to do it because nobody would believe that it was a real illness, or if they did, would seek to take advantage of it. And the doctor told Mao that if he went on for more than half an hour in the conversation with Nixon, he wouldn't be responsible for the consequences. In fact, he went on for about fifty minutes, and it explains why whenever Nixon raised a substantive issue, Mao kept saying, "This has to be done by Zhou Enlai and others." And partly, it was that since the Shanghai Communiqué had not yet been finally agreed to, he did not want to be associated with a possible failure. But apparently, he had been extremely ill.

Could you tell when you were sitting down with him that he was in poor health?

No, but in the later meetings with him, after this trip, we could see him getting more and more frail.

We had a meeting with him in 1975 preparing for the Ford visit, and at that time he had great difficulty speaking. He would croak something, and they would write their understanding of it on a piece of paper and hold it up for him.

I also think it was interesting that Zhou Enlai's demeanor changed when he was sitting with Mao as opposed to being on his own.

When Zhou negotiated with me, he was a sovereign personality who was in complete command of his side of the room. When Mao was present, he was totally deferential. I don't recall any interjection. He would just maybe throw in a word, but even that I couldn't remember precisely.

So the negotiation really was between Mao and Nixon, not all four of you?

At the summit, there was no real negotiation because Mao refused to discuss any substantive issues. The conversation between Mao and Nixon was on very general principles. The Shanghai Communiqué was negotiated between Zhou and the Chinese vice foreign minister and me. Zhou reviewed with Nixon the evolution of specific issues and countries, but Mao said some very important things. One, that he was not interested in the immediate unification of China. He said, "We can wait. They are a bunch of revolutionaries." That was a very important assurance at that time. And then he said he'd come to the view that he would rather deal with Western conservatives than with Western left people, which meant that this was an instruction to the people reading this transcript that he meant for the negotiation to succeed. He was extremely affable with Nixon, but there was no real negotiation.

What were your impressions of Brezhnev and Gromyko, and perhaps Dobrynin?

Well, first Dobrynin. He was a superb professional. He knew his subject. He knew America, which is not always true of Russian diplomats. And he handled his job with extraordinary skill. He, I think, as the years went by, became invested to some extent in the U.S.-Soviet dialogue. But he never went beyond—so far as we could tell—the instructions from Moscow. So he never did what American negotiators sometimes do, which is to advance a personal negotiating position that he would try to sell to his government. That he never did. But he was extremely skillful in keeping contact with many elements in Washington. I grew to respect him greatly. And I occasionally scheduled a meeting in which I said, "Now, let's just think out loud to each other. Let's not talk in terms of what our instructions are, but how do we assess what we are doing." And that sometimes was successful, and sometimes he was more restrained. But if you look over the decades, a decade and a half of service, he was just about the best ambassador you could imagine, because he was a strong defender of the views of his country, but he had enough flexibility to understand our way of thinking. And he knew America well enough to know what was possible in our system.

What about Gromyko?

Gromyko was a diplomat's diplomat. He got into that job by rigid adherence to the line of the Politburo. In Russia, there was a separation of knowledge so that the foreign minister was generally not informed about the thinking, in detail, of the military. So I probably knew more, as secretary of state, about Russian military dispositions and Russian capabilities than Gromyko did, until he became a member of the Politburo.

But in the period before he became a member of the Politburo, there was one occasion where he extrapolated the formal position of the Russian government into asking for space for a missile that our intelligence had never discovered. And so we didn't know what this negotiation was about. And he kept doggedly pressing for the theoretical right to build a missile of dimensions that we had never heard of. During a break, a Russian general who was on his staff went up to me and said, "If you defer this discussion until tomorrow morning, I think we can have a fuller view of it." So the next morning, we went back to that topic, and we never heard of that missile again.

He had a good sense of humor, too. He had quadruple negative sentences in English and so on.

Yes, he had a very understated and somewhat complex sense of humor, and all of it put forward with a very dour face. And he was a great genius in constructing sentences that had a double negative and sounded unbelievably complicated. But I don't remember any of the precise sentences now.

What about Brezhnev? Did he play the key role?

On the organization chart he played the key role, and he won the power struggle in the sense of replacing Khrushchev with a triumvirate and then emerging as the strongest member of the triumvirate. We met him at the end of his life, really. When we first met him, he was ebullient and dynamic and controlling on the Soviet side, never very intellectual, but there was always a heavy emotional aspect. He was much more personal than the other Soviet leaders that we met.

He was a heavy smoker, and his doctors were trying to get him to quit. And he had a little gun that was supposed to go off whenever he violated the doctors' orders and lit a cigarette. He spent a lot of time playing with that gun. Because you have to remember, each of us had to sit through the translations of lengthy statements of the other. And usually, after one of my statements, when the interpreter was talking, Brezhnev would go off and walk around the room and sign papers, because our meetings were generally in his office or in the office of the Politburo. There was a desk at the end of it and a long table around which we negotiated. So he was very personable.

I always thought, in retrospect, that he was a kind of forerunner of [president Mikhail] Gorbachev, that he knew somehow that the system was screwed up, and somehow he had to make peace with us. But it was still too rigid for him, or maybe he wasn't imaginative enough.

There was one amusing moment during the European Security Conference. He had had a stroke a few months earlier, and he had strength basically for only two hours of working time in any one meeting. That's in 1975. We had basically used up the meeting time in talking about SALT. He was trying to break up the meeting. This was under President Ford. At the end of the planned time, President Ford said, "We still haven't discussed the Middle East." Brezhnev said, "Let Henry handle it. He can talk to Gromyko about it later." And you could see that Gromyko was expiring in his seat, and it didn't happen that way, either. But Brezhnev was just trying to get out of the room.

What about Le Duc Tho?

Can I tell what I said to Le Duc Tho when I needed to go to the bathroom? I said, "Objective necessity requires me to ask for a break." And he then spent forty-five minutes explaining to me that I didn't have the right to use communist jargon.

He used to get headaches at an appropriate time, too. Remember that?

Yes, when he wanted to waste time. Still, he was impressive— I mean, considering what he was up against with us. We could have smashed him any time that we got impatient. He was dealing with a superpower with such capacity, never lost his composure, torturing us with extreme skill and extreme politeness. He never said anything that would make you personally angry. It was such that the procedure felt like a surgeon operating on you. You knew very well what he was doing, but your only remedy was to worsen your own position.

There was one other great moment. He had the same opening speech as part of his psychological warfare of exhausting us. Practically every day, it was the same opening speech. It was about forty minutes. You had to listen to it like an opening prayer, and it didn't change. And one key sentence in it was, "If you make a big effort, we will make a big effort." So one day he said, "If you make a big effort, we'll make an effort." And just to break the monotony, I said, "Mr. Special Advisor, have I noticed that you have changed your phraseology here?" And he said, "I'm so glad you noticed it, because yesterday we made a big effort, and you only made an effort." You remember?

Absolutely.

TEN

The Foreign Policy Process

A sound process to formulate and execute foreign policy does not guarantee success, but a defective one all but ensures failure.

There is no magic formula. Past administrations, with varying success, have followed approaches dominated by either the White House, the State Department, or with the two in balance.

There are, however, two prerequisites: the system must reflect the president's priorities and must allow all concerned actors to weigh in with their views. No doubt, President Nixon centered control in the White House and entrusted the most sensitive negotiations to Kissinger. But the relevant agencies were called upon for background, analysis, and recommendations—and these were woven into the fabrics of the diplomatic achievements.

Whatever the process, on the most critical decisions, it is lonely at the top for any president grappling with portentous options. As Kissinger wrote his parents from postwar

Germany, "Real dilemmas are difficulties of the soul, provoking agonies."

* * *

All of this gets us into the NSC system, which we discussed before, but you may want to do final reflections on what suits any president. How much is it keyed to the president himself? Are there some general principles for this system? How did it work for Nixon in terms of the pluses and minuses?

I think it's important to repeat that when Nixon started, when I was assigned as national security advisor, I had no fixed idea of what the NSC system would be like. Nixon assigned General Goodpaster to me to help design it, because he had been on Eisenhower's staff during the war and then in the White House.

Again, the major impact of Eisenhower on Nixon's NSC system as it evolved came from his view that the State Department should not be put in charge of day-to-day interdepartmental operations. That was the reason why the White House became the chairman of these interdepartmental committees. And that system has, in fact, been maintained for all the years since then, for the same reason that Eisenhower recommended it. The debates in the NSC were generally between Cabinet members. To designate one of them as chairman of an interdepartmental committee skewers the process. The NSC office representing the president is in the best position of impartiality. Eisenhower also thought that the State Department was not well organized for such a role.

Could you reflect a little bit on the division between State and NSC and how much the president should delegate foreign policy?

If I were teaching a seminar, I would say the secretary of state ought to conduct foreign policy and become the originator of all policy, and that he should be the chief spokesman and all of the proper things. But if you look at experience, I know no administration in which it operated quite this way. The closest to it was [James] Baker and [George H. W.] Bush, because they had been lifetime friends. But even there, when Bush wanted to restart relations with China after Tiananmen, he didn't send Baker. He sent [Brent] Scowcroft. And the reason is that there are some things that are so special to the position of the president that the security advisor is more often than not used in those conditions. It can be done with the secretary of state, but the secretary of state has nearly 200 countries to deal with. He has dozens of conferences that he must attend to show the American presence. So that as a practical matter, this abstract idea that the security advisor just sits in the outer office and produces options and the secretary of state runs it all almost never happens in practice.

I agree with that, but wouldn't you agree that the center of gravity depends a little bit on the president? For example, you and Ford, and [Ronald] Reagan and [George] Shultz?

It depends entirely on the president. But if you don't have a strong security advisor, who has a view of the range of existing options and who simply, or largely, controls the flow of papers in and out of the White House, then you get a bigger role for the various departments. It is in the interest of good policy to have a security advisor with developed views.

Because if you don't have that, then the bureaucracy is apt to engulf you. But the security advisor needs to avoid acting primarily as an advocate.

And what you've implied is the bureaucracy is not where the creative new ideas are going to come from.

This is no reflection on the bureaucracy, but in practice there are *x* thousand cables that come into Washington a day. They need a response, so the system is geared to dealing with current issues. It has proved almost impossible to break through this system. We did it in the Nixon and Ford administrations by making Winston the head of the Policy Planning Staff. That alone wouldn't have done it. But I had Winston as an integral part of my personal staff, so everybody in the building knew that I would make no recommendation without Winston. So that drew the Policy Planning Staff into a more operational role than they would normally play. Normally, they write abstract papers that are hard to bring to bear on the issue that is before you.

So ideally you should have a secretary of state and a security advisor and a president who are harmonious in this, and you can act as a team. That's absolutely the ideal. And to a certain extent in Bush 41 that existed, because Bush was a close friend of Baker's and Scowcroft had worked with Bush in the Nixon Administration. So that worked.

Is it personalities as much as policies?

It's partly personalities. When you get to the Cabinet level, you are used to having your own way, or you don't get there. And if you don't have your way and feel thwarted, you are resentful.

So it bleeds over into policies.

Inevitably. And it is not unknown that presidents don't discourage this by playing off their various advisors against each other. Franklin Roosevelt was a master at that, to take an historic example.

How about the other agencies? Particularly as the world has evolved, the Defense Department, the economic agencies, and CIA and so on. Where do they fit into this?

The CIA needs to be an absolutely integral part of the process, because they shape it in part by their assessments. Others may differ with their assessments, but the CIA was the one unit in the government that theoretically had no policy objectives. Their job was to give us the best judgment of what the situation was. Therefore, the Nixon NSC was closely tied in with the CIA, not so much on hot news, but mostly on where is this process going? What do they think they are doing on the other side?

We had one debate early in the administration on some Soviet missile developments. And we had access to all the technical information, but we wanted to understand whether the Soviets might be aiming at a first-strike capability by developing high accuracy. I called the analysts into the Situation Room to tell me how they came to their conclusions. The CIA leaders did not like that, because their view was the CIA director delivered the analysis. He did not want his staff to be checked on how they reached it.

Now, economics: I realized that I did not have technical economic capability, and I didn't try to acquire it. I tried to have a very close relationship with [Commerce Secretary]

Pete Peterson and even [Treasury Secretary] John Connally in order to understand. I didn't second-guess their measures from the financial point of view, but I tried to have a position on the impact of their measures on the political situation. In that way, I wound up in a direct role on one occasion, when Nixon met with [Georges] Pompidou, the French president, in the Azores. Connally was the secretary of treasury, and he said he didn't want to be involved in making concessions, so I was the sacrificial lamb. I was sent over to see Pompidou, who was a banker. I said to Pompidou, "You have a huge advantage in your knowledge, and I have a huge advantage in my ignorance, because beyond the position I'm bringing you, there is chaos in my mind, I can't modify it."

But as a general rule, I tried to understand the foreign policy implications of Treasury positions. If I had a problem with the foreign policy implications, I would take it to Nixon. But I had very compatible Treasury and Commerce secretaries, compatible with his system, because Connally was a very strong man, and both were very thoughtful.

But in today's world, with economic power being relatively much more important than it was, you might have to think of this system differently.

Yes. For example, in a TPP [Trans-Pacific Partnership] negotiation, as security advisor, I would turn that over to the most highly qualified person I could find on the day-to-day stuff and only reserve my views to the "what are we trying to do here" question.

It involves the general impact on our presence in Asia, not only the economic dimension.

On that, I would think I knew the political situation more closely than the economists.

When you were dealing with the Soviet Union, China, the Middle East, were you considering the economic implications of foreign policy or the foreign policy implications of economic developments? How were you putting those together?

Well, that situation was quite different from today because when we opened to China, our trade with China was less than our trade with Honduras. And Russia was also a self-contained unit. One of our efforts was, which today it's hard to imagine, I tried to get Russia to sell oil on the open market as a threat to OPEC after the 1973 war and oil embargo. I tried to find arrangements where Russia could pay for grain and things like that with oil. Our reasoning was that if there were more oil on the market, it would depress the price. But it was violently opposed by the security elements in the government, and by the oil companies also. So we never could make that work. But Winston is right: Russia and China were not major economic players in the Nixon Administration. So we had to be aware of economics, but it wasn't a day-to-day concern.

Now, the Defense Department is staffed by individuals where executing orders is a way of life, so my general view, put ironically—not exactly correct, but pretty close—is if the White House gives an order to the Defense Department, there's an 80 percent chance of it being executed and 100 percent chance of something like it being executed. If the White House gives an order to the State Department, it is the opening of a negotiation.

Except when someone wears both hats, like the NSC advisor and the secretary of state—then it works a little better!

Yes it does! But the basic view of the Defense Department is oriented to the commander in chief, whereas the State Department is organized toward the secretary of state. The basic instinct of the State Department is that they have spent a lifetime studying political and diplomatic problems, so that if they are ordered to do something they don't agree with particularly, they have to be given a chance to offer alternatives. And that's correct, but there is not the same automaticity you see in Defense built into the State Department system because it's more reflective. Not so much depends on immediate execution.

So there is a difference in dealing with the two. In leading the State Department, it is important for the president and the security advisor and of course decisive for the secretary to bring the department along to his way of thinking. If you do it always by orders, it will never work because they will not be part of what you think. So an important part of leadership is to educate your department.

On public opinion, Hubert Humphrey called me once when there was debate and criticism of us in Washington, and he said, "This is a Beltway phenomenon. You get out in the country and make your case to the public. In the public, they take you very seriously. And if every congressman sees you going through his state, this will give you a lot of influence." He said, "When you come to Minnesota, I'll go around with you," and he was a presidential candidate that year. Unthinkable today that this would happen in the present climate. We took it seriously. I think we made forty-one speeches in different states. And every state to which we went, I made a speech, I met with leadership groups, I gave a press conference. And it was rarely reported in Washington.

But you dominated the local media.

I think it was a tremendous help in getting our policy established in the public mind.

And also speeches, even if they weren't read that carefully here, they were read in foreign capitals, and you forced the bureaucracy in America to come to decisions by generating the draft.

There was a big conference at the UN where we used the fact of a secretarial speech to outline a whole series of measures that we were prepared to take. And it took two hours to read that speech. It was drafted while I was negotiating the Syrian shuttle. Winston, who was with me, kept rewriting the speech all during the trip. So I'm just trying to describe how we operated. I'm not saying that this is something that can be used as a model, except that the key elements of it were necessary and in some way had to be done.

On the economic side, when we had a problem that we thought affected the political alignment of countries, we would try to give a speech on the subject, even if it was a largely economic problem. We had one exercise where we advocated a floor price for oil production to encourage alternative sources. It doesn't matter whether we were right or wrong on the economics; I made it on a subject usually handled by Treasury to illustrate that.

What about the role of Congress, what about its responsibilities?

This is part of the same thing: you had to win over the hearts and minds of the people, and you used the speech-making process, traveling around the country, to get the public support.

We had to move the Congress. My position was never that of a typical secretary because of Vietnam and Watergate, and we faced enormous tensions. So with the Congress, we tried to do a lot of conceptual briefing.

You did this with the press, too, in backgrounders as well.

This was as secretary of state or as security advisor?

I started them as national security advisor. The security advisor doesn't testify before Congress, so I told [William] Fulbright that if he invited the [Senate Foreign Relations] Committee to his house for a drink, I'd show up, and we could have a discussion that way. And that went on for several years, and, of course, Nixon knew about it and encouraged it.

We put a lot of emphasis on conceptual briefings, on telling them, really quite accurately, where we were going. But then much occurred during the period of Watergate. And then some of the Democratic leaders got the idea that if Nixon was for détente, a little tension might not be too bad, so the lines were shifting.

Yes. You were the doves, and they were the hawks!

But we had one great advantage, that there were a lot of serious senators who had been in office for a long time and who were very much guided by the principle of the national interest. So you could call in people like [Richard] Russell, or [John] Stennis, or the chairmen of the various committees and say, "Your country needs this," and this wouldn't be taken as a PR trick. Two or three times a year you could get at least a substantial reaction. You shouldn't abuse this, but there were people to whom you could talk that way.

As opposed to congressmen or senators who are looking out for their own political futures.

This is as opposed to having rigid political lines, rigid party lines. In the Nixon Administration, with all the problems we had with the Congress, it was absolutely imperative to exchange views. It was a different Washington then. On Sunday nights, [journalist] Joe Alsop would have a dinner inviting Republican and Democratic leaders and me. That took some of the poison out of these debates.

Do you think that's a good lesson for today, for politics today, which has become so partisan?

Well, the trouble is that, then, people were living in Washington while the current Congress people are not living in Washington. They go home on weekends. And there was a sense of commonality. Joe Alsop as a center. Polly Wisner, Kay Graham even. It was understood that what went on at these dinners never got into the newspapers. It created a kind of dialogue, a permanent dialogue that was a huge asset, and which, as far as I can tell, is not taking place today.

No, it's not taking place today. Neither are there backgrounders with the media, or talking between the Right and Left, or even within one's own party.

I think your backgrounders with the media were very important. You really spent a lot of time doing this. And again, they were conceptual more than tactical.

Well, if you look at the time we spent on my speeches . . .

And the foreign policy reports that you wrote.

Take the time we spent on the speeches and the amount of time we spent on backgrounders; they must be available. Every Friday, for the first few years, I gave a backgrounder on Vietnam and other things. Confidentiality was never violated. It was like a Harvard seminar. I would give them good explanation.

And I can give you another example. I was once on Air Force One, and they had a press group at the back of the plane. I went back and chatted with them. We were going to Salzburg to meet with Sadat. And when we landed, Murrey Marder of the *Washington Post,* who was a senior guy, called me up and said, "You should know that the press pool got you totally screwed up. They're quoting you as saying things which I know from traveling with you, you do not believe, and they're gonna be a mess." So I said, "What can I do about it?" He then said, "You can do nothing because you're not supposed to know what's in the pool report. The best thing you can do," he said, "is to call an open press conference, and I'll ask you a question relevant to that subject, and then you can spell out what I know you really mean. Then they will have to quote it." Can you conceive of this happening today?

No, you could never do that today. They would be rushing to print and try to make you look foolish!

Talk to us about the Nixon-Kissinger legacy. Not just the foreign policy with China, the Soviet Union, arms control, and the Middle East, but also the political legacy. And you also influenced a whole generation of future diplomats and leaders.

Well, I am proud of the people who worked with me, and then maintained forty years of public service in every administration. We didn't set out to do that, but this is what happened, maybe because we were not a partisan group. One of the high points of my experience in government, as I look back on it, was when we went into Cambodia, and Winston was thinking of leaving. At least I thought he was thinking of leaving. I called him in and I said, "Winston, you have a choice. You can go out there and run around with a placard, or you can work with me, and we might end the Vietnam War."

And Winston chose to stay with me even though his friends were mostly on the other side. And then there came that point where the Vietnamese accepted a proposal that Nixon had made nine months earlier, which was the breakthrough in the negotiations. When the meeting was ending, I turned to Winston and said, "We have done it," and shook hands. So that was the atmosphere in which we were working. We never thought this is a Republican versus Democratic thing, nor did Nixon. Whatever maneuvers he may have made in the domestic field, in the foreign field he was dominated by the national interest.

And as you look back, did you know that you were just setting down a forty-, fifty-year legacy when you were doing this?

No. I mean, if you read my writings before, I knew the problem, but I do not recall conversations in which we said to ourselves, "How is this going to look in fifty years?" We did try to ask ourselves, "Where is this going for peace?"

So I'd like to think that what I have tried consistently to do is to think in long-range terms and in the national interest, but in the national interest related to the national interests of other countries. Because if you assert only your interests, without linking them to the interests of others, you will not be able to sustain your efforts. It's important to know the national interests. It's important to know how to use them. There are a number of achievements that we've talked about that aren't for me to list. But if you look at the major policies in the Middle East, the major policies toward Asia, the major policies toward Europe, arms control, the Nixon period had a big role in shaping them.

———•———

ELEVEN

Strategy

The lack of an overall strategy makes one a prisoner of events. The most important bond between President Nixon and Kissinger was their shared strategic approach. While continually assessing tactics, they focused on where they were headed for the long run.

This approach infused American policy on the major issues. It moved us from mutual isolation to a dramatic opening. From dealing with one communist country to dealing with several. From a tense nuclear stalemate to a steadier relationship. From a tormenting quagmire to an honorable peace. From the sway of Soviet arms to American diplomacy.

They did not always succeed. They made mistakes. But by looking over the horizon, linking issues and relationships, melding incentives and pressures, they made major strides not only on discrete issues but in reshaping the international landscape.

* * *

We've had forty years to reflect on the foreign policy of President Nixon. Looking back, how do you see that legacy today?

The fundamental contribution of Nixon was to establish a pattern of thinking on foreign policy, which is seminal. The traditional thinking of American foreign policy has been that issues could be segmented into the resolution of individual problems—in fact that the solution of problems was the issue. So we would get involved in a situation that seemed to threaten our survival or some other vital interest but rarely over concepts of world order.

Nixon was, except for the Founding Fathers and, I would say, Teddy Roosevelt, the American president who thought of foreign policy as grand strategy. To him, foreign policy was the structural improvement of the relationship of countries to each other in a way that the balancing of their self-interests would promote global peace and the security of the United States.

And he thought about that in relatively long-range terms.

Give us some examples of this kind of strategic, long-range thinking.

Of course, the most obvious one is China. If you look at what Nixon said about China, and what was said in the foreign policy reports that were produced under Nixon's aegis, he addressed the problem of China from the point of view of world order, not from the point of view of any particular crisis, nor from the point of view of Vietnam, even though he saw an impact on Vietnam.

His view was that by getting China involved in the international system, the whole pattern of international politics would be transformed, because all other countries would then have to consider the impact of China in terms of the new dispensation. He calculated that, insofar as the relationship between China and the United States would generate confidence in each other's positions, we might produce a situation in which America would be closer to China and Russia than they were to each other. We therefore would have a strong bargaining position. He also thought that as the American public's perception of the prospect of peace changed, our domestic sense of purpose would be strengthened.

Another example is the Middle East. Very early in the administration, we decided that we would try to expel Russian military domination and influence in the region. And in fact, I said so. Using the word "expel" was badly chosen from a domestic point of view, but it was what we intended to do. Our strategy was to demonstrate, in all these negotiations that were going on, that Russian military pressure or Soviet military presence would not be permitted to decide the outcome.

We thought that somewhere along the line, some Arab country would jump ship and decide that American diplomacy, and not Russian arms, was needed to solve the problem. We hung in there for four years until this was achieved in the face of criticism, especially from Europe.

So, correct me if I'm wrong, but you were thinking of this when you came into the administration, even before the 1973 Yom Kippur War?

This decision was made in '69.

So even then, when the Soviet Union was the dominant power in the Arab world, shaping events in the Arab world, you and

Nixon could conceive of a time when the United States would take the place of the Soviet Union as the dominating shaper of events?

The Soviet Union wasn't totally dominating because there was Israel, which we had a special relationship with, and there were countries like Jordan and Saudi Arabia that were not pro-Soviet. But in the larger states like Egypt and Syria and Iraq, the Soviet Union was the practically exclusive arms supplier and sort of the diplomatically dominant one.

But since we did not think they were capable of achieving a military solution, we concluded that if we could demonstrate that reality, sooner or later some Arab country would move toward the American diplomatic option. And, in fact, Sadat expelled the Soviet advisors in 1972, which was a signal to us. We needed some time to develop that signal.

It seems to me also that the president and you recognized that, although very strong supporters of Israel, you wanted to be in a position where you could broker between the two sides, whereas the Russians were really the advocates for the Arab world alone. So the United States would have great influence as being an honest intermediary even though strongly supporting Israel. Isn't that fair to say?

It is fair to say that we would not tolerate the military defeat of Israel by Soviet arms, or by anybody else's arms. Therefore, we would create a situation where a diplomatic solution had to be found if one wanted progress at all.

So when you came into government, you and Nixon had a strategic vision of where you wanted the world to go, or where America could help shape events with China, the Soviet

Union, arms control, the Middle East. What were the concrete steps you were going to take to make that happen? To be proactive? To bring it along more quickly?

You know, I hadn't met Nixon until the beginning of the administration. Yet, as it happened, he and I had developed very parallel views. But it was not that we came in and said we know the ten next steps that we're going to take.

In the case of China, we knew that we wanted to open to China, but we did not know how to do it at the beginning. We tried all kinds of emissaries who we thought might pass a message.

In the Middle East, the strategic objective was to demonstrate that you could not achieve diplomatic progress by the pressure of Soviet arms. So in the various crises that occurred in the period leading up to the '73 war, our position was always to convey to the Arabs that we are willing and eager to be a diplomatic intermediary, but we will not do it in response to Soviet military pressure.

What were your strategic objectives with the Soviet Union? Détente, arms control?

Our strategic objective was to prevent the Soviet Union from becoming the hegemonic country. Nixon came into office when the Soviet army had just occupied Czechoslovakia six months earlier, and one of the strategic events of our period was that forty-two Russian divisions were deployed on the Chinese border. So the use of Soviet military pressure was a feature of the Cold War world to be dealt with. Nixon also began by saying that he was open to an era of negotiations, and we agreed to the opening of arms control negotiations on strategic nuclear weapons. We were never happy to have a military negotiation that was separated from a political one. Throughout, we tried to link them to restrained political conduct.

You've written and you've alluded to Immanuel Kant's belief, that sometimes you have very difficult choices between morals and objectives. For example, on détente with the Soviet Union you had to balance, as you put it, "the defense of freedom" with coexisting with a nuclear adversary. Could you elaborate a bit on that balance?

In the American public discussion, the issue is often put this way: you have the choice between coexistence and détente or . . . But then the question is . . . or what? The nuclear equilibrium in a way condemns you to some kind of coexistence.

So the question was, could you elaborate a principle of coexistence which preserved the safety of free peoples and at the same time created an opportunity where, in the process of negotiations, our political relations could be improved at least to a point where in crises the two countries were in sufficient communication with each other that they wouldn't escalate into an all-out war automatically?

Nixon managed this to a substantial degree. The general policy was to be very tough in resistance to Soviet overt military movement, but to do it in a context where the Soviet decision-makers could always calculate they were giving up the possibility of a long-term improved relationship with the United States.

And when one reads now in the documents that have been published of the internal Soviet discussions throughout the '73 war, the Soviets, on the one hand, were tempted to reinforce their Arab allies, but at the same time they were also concerned with not wrecking the relationship with the United States totally.

So when we not only matched but considerably exceeded for Israel whatever support the Soviets had given to their allies, then a diplomatic solution had to be found first between us and the Soviet Union, and then with us as mediators between Israel and the Arab states, and we, at the end of that war, were the negotiators of the cease-fire.

We produced three agreements between Arabs and Israel—two with Egypt and one with Syria—in an eighteen-month period. That was not due to negotiating skills. Whatever negotiating skills existed were made possible because we had shaped a strategic situation where all the parties in the Middle East, if they wanted to achieve their objectives, had to deal with us.

A point on the legacy of Nixon. When he came in, the credibility of the U.S. abroad, or the feeling that the U.S. could do anything active or dramatic, was weak because of the Vietnam preoccupation. The mood of the American people was pretty bleak, and no matter how the Vietnam issue came out it was going to be at best ambiguous.

As a result of the dramatic initiatives we've been discussing, it seems to me that there was a major change in the morale of Americans, in their confidence in what we could do on the world stage. And abroad, the U.S. was now more credible, its diplomacy freed up and dynamic.

I believe these count as remarkable achievements. Would you agree with that?

Yes. Such shifts have happened at the end of overwhelming victories in a war, but rarely have happened due to the forging of a diplomatic framework where more or less equal countries were dealing with each other and the United States was in a key permanent position to influence their actions. This was a result of the emphasis that had been put on developing a strategic design.

For example, as we have discussed, six months after Nixon came in, there were a series of border clashes between Soviet and Chinese military forces, and we analyzed them, thinking at first that the Chinese were the more radical and therefore the most likely aggressor. We then became convinced that for that period the Soviets were the most likely aggressors.

So the question was, what does America do? We had no diplomatic relations. We had not even made contact with China yet; even though we had tried, we had not succeeded. So we decided that if you don't know what to do in a situation, support the weaker against the stronger, because you don't want to encourage aggression.

And there was a meeting at the Cabinet level where Nixon pronounced that principle. He said that if the Soviet Union attacked China, with which we had no diplomatic relations or contact, we would lean toward China, because we did not want the Soviet Union to become the absolutely dominant country.

I can't say that every colleague was smitten by that idea, but a president who knows what he wants usually gets his way. And then the Soviet attack didn't occur, but we conducted ourselves and conveyed through messages and through public statements that a general decision to move toward China had been made.

When you look at the Sino-Soviet border conflict of 1969, why would Nixon want to get involved anyway? Why not just ignore it? After all, that was the Soviet world, the communist world.

We had no particular interest in the border dispute, but we had an interest to prevent the Soviet Union, after occupying Czechoslovakia, from succeeding in dominating China. If that happened, the Soviets might be able to achieve a dominant position simply by military threats.

The border clashes also made clear that the Chinese had an incentive to work with us because of their fear of the Soviet Union.

Yes. The Chinese decided to move toward the United States, even though it took about two more years to bring it to a point of an actual contact. Nixon would never have been interested in the details of the border dispute. He would have been interested in the strategic and historic consequences of a Soviet victory over China in the wake of the Soviet occupation of Czechoslovakia and the American entanglement in Vietnam.

Acknowledgments

I greatly appreciate the dedicated role of Geoff Shepard and Jonathan Movroydis of the Nixon Foundation in the planning, production, and technical polishing of the videos from which this book is drawn.

I am also grateful to Dr. Kissinger's superb staff. Theresa Amantea, Sarah Chandler, Jessee LePorin, and Meredith Potter shepherded us all through the video and book stages, carved out innumerable meetings from Kissinger's insane schedule, and juggled his competing requirements. As for Theresa, she also somehow met the awesome challenge of deciphering and rendering the mysterious Kissinger scribblings.

My warm thanks and admiration also go to my agent Andrew Wylie, renowned representative of luminous fiction and nonfiction authors, including Dr. Kissinger. His strong team, featuring Katie Cacouris and Jessica Calagione, steered me through this process with great skill.

I am honored to be published by the distinguished firm of St. Martin's Press. And I am indebted to Adam Bellow, who championed this book and whose All Points imprint is stimulating the rational political and cultural dialogue sorely needed in America. Alan Bradshaw, Katherine Haigler, Kevin Reilly, and Bill Warhop have shaped, polished, and projected this volume with formidable talent and dedication. Also thanks to Sara Beth Haring, Leah Johanson, Paul Hochman, and Joy Gannon at St. Martin's Press.

Above all, I want to express my deep gratitude to K.T. McFarland, a co-producer of this volume. We collaborated seamlessly for four years, from steering the foreign policy panels through the Kissinger interviews to turning the video transcripts into this book. She played a central role in cleaning up the recorded written text of the videos, shaping the Foreword, and posing questions to Kissinger. She has been an excellent moderator, interrogator, and wordsmith, as well as a congenial partner.

As conveyed in the Foreword, my profound thanks to Henry Kissinger.

Index